W9-ASG-492

A Machine Called Indomitable

Dear Colleague,

I am sending you this book so you can share with me the exciting story of the development of MR scanning and what it holds for the future of medicine.

Raymond Damadian, M. D.
President and Chairman of the Board
FONAR Corporation
Melville, New York

Also by the Author

The Traders
The Biggest Company on Earth
The Hidden Minority
A Month at the Brickyard

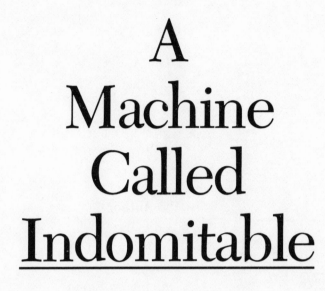

A Machine Called Indomitable

by

Sonny Kleinfield

Times BOOKS

Copyright © 1985 by Sonny Kleinfield

All rights reserved under International and Pan-American Copyright
Conventions. Published in the United States by Times Books,
a division of Random House, Inc., New York, and simultaneously
in Canada by Random House of Canada Limited, Toronto.

Library of Congress Cataloging-in-Publication Data

Kleinfield, Sonny.
A machine called indomitable.

Includes index.
1. Damadian, R. (Raymond), 1936-   . 2. Medical
research personnel—United States—Biography.
3. Magnetic resonance imaging.   4. Cancer—Diagnosis.
I. Title.
RC78.7.N83D365   1985   616.07′5   85-40270
ISBN 0-8129-1234-9

Designed by Stephanie Blumenthal
Manufactured in the United States of America
9 8 7 6 5 4 3 2

For Susan

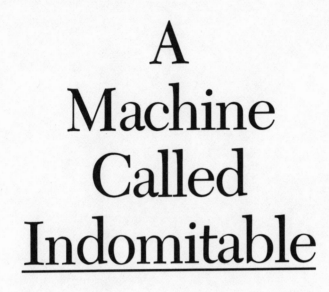

A
Machine
Called
Indomitable

ONE

On the day that his stomach first began to bother him, Raymond Damadian was annoyed and nothing more. After all, he hardly ever got sick, and there seemed to be no particular reason for the pain. At any rate, the distress subsided, and matters of greater urgency than his belly laid claim to his attention. On subsequent days, however, the ache reappeared, and it conspired to produce some disquieting anxieties in him. "It was not an excruciating pain" is how Damadian described it to others. "It was just a pain that made me uneasy. It made me wonder, Hey, what's wrong with me?"

This was in the middle 1960s, when Damadian was a postdoctoral fellow at Harvard University, framing a future in medical research. "It was a high-pressure place to be. There was a lot of competition. I thought I might have an ulcer, but there weren't full-fledged ulcer symptoms. And the pain was associated with high acidity. Acid would come up and I could taste it in my mouth." What would almost invariably bring on the bellyache was coffee. "I'd be fine. Then I'd have two cups of coffee and it would come roaring back." Damadian was firmly attached to coffee and found himself unable to forgo it entirely, though he forced himself to cut back his consumption. Wine and chocolate would aggravate the pain as well; they disappeared from his diet. He discovered that he would find a certain amount of relief when he ate. Though he had never eaten sparingly, he began to dine with more abandon. The remedy was fairly quickly reflected in his waistline. For the first time in his life he became a little thick in the middle.

The stomachache continued to bother him sporadically after he left Harvard and was drafted into the service. Frightful thoughts slowly crept into his mind. He had never been sick before, and now he had these baffling pains. When they persisted for days at a time, his flesh would contract with fear. Fears blossom quickly when you're the one who's sick. He found himself surrendering to the sort of paranoia that was all too common among people stricken by an inexplicable ache. Was it possible? Could it be that he had cancer?

After the service, when he joined the faculty of the Downstate Medical Center, a part of the State University of New York, the gastric pain changed its character. It now seemed to wrap around his stomach, like a band. It felt as if he had cinched his belt too tight. When he bent over, it would get worse. In his mind, it was not only possible but more and more apparent that he had cancer. He became increasingly sullen. One day he paid a nervous visit to the director of gastrointestinal services at Downstate, a strapping, moon-faced man who was very sure of himself. A series of X-rays was taken of Damadian's stomach. There was no evidence of anything untoward: no tumors, no ulcers, nothing. After seeing the X-rays, the doctor reported to him that nothing seemed to be wrong. Perhaps, he went on to suggest, his problem was aerophagia, or air-swallowing. Otherwise, as far as he could see, he was perfectly all right.

Damadian could have been convincingly cast as the gumshoe in an impossibly complex mystery novel, the constantly prying sleuth who never accepts anything anyone says, especially if it makes sense. He had pleasant good looks, with a broad brow and direct and friendly eyes. He was a garrulous and expansive man of promptly revealed opinions, announced in a voice of conviction and penetration. He was forceful and righteous; the Bible was one of the touchstones of his life. A few years before, he had attended an evangelical crusade at

Madison Square Garden, at which he "gave his life to Christ."
He had a candor that few could surpass. His blunt remarks
seemed to win him a good many admirers but an equally sizable swarm of enemies. Within the tough outer sheath, however, there was a restlessness, a yearning for something missing, and he would vacillate between moods of frustration and
elation. His notions conformed with those of very few, and he
was, even at this early date, always finding murkinesses and
shortcomings in fellow scientists. His ambitions at times were
so great that they seemed irrational. At almost all points of his
career, he found himself at odds with the establishment.

Now Damadian sat and listened with displeasure to the
Downstate doctor's diagnosis. Ludicrous, he thought. Level-
ing his gaze, he protested that something was wrong. His
stomach was killing him. For all he knew, he had cancer and
was shortly doomed to die. The doctor's rather huffy response
was: "Look, you haven't lost fifty pounds, have you? You
haven't lost your appetite, have you? Then why are you pest-
ering me?"

Damadian, whenever he remembers this incident, works
up a suitable amount of irritation, expressed in a flush of color
in his face. "Well, I was peeved. The reason I went to him was
to have him find out what was going on before I lost my appetite and before I lost fifty pounds. Before I was an absolute
wreck. Before I was dead. I said to myself that they've got to
come up with a better way of detecting things. I mean, this
was primitive. If you didn't have something big enough to
shove a barium swallow halfway across the abdomen, they
couldn't find it."

His stomach disturbances eventually moderated, forever
unexplained. The mysterious experience, however, stimulated Damadian's discontent. It revealed a circumstance that
he found abhorrent. He wondered, could man not come up
with some better way to make the body transparent and un-

ravel its secrets of life and death? Though it was simply an aimless thought, the seed of an idea was planted that someday perhaps he could discover a device that would make it possible to detect disease as never before. "I was irritated and frustrated at the technology," he would subsequently say. "I thought there should be a better technology. At that point, I felt it was a problem that I ought to solve and that probably nobody else would solve. When a serious problem occurs and you get down to the wire, I have no confidence in other people to work it out. I feel that most people who are charged with solving things are just wandering around in the playground of science."

At that moment, of course, Damadian seemed to be doing nothing more than spinning implausible daydreams. What he was thinking about was a wondrous machine based on some uninvented technology that would spot the remotest trouble signs early, when disease could still be tamed, something that would work with such precision that it would transform diagnosis from an inscrutable art to an exact science—something, in short, that would be every bit as momentous a discovery as the X-ray itself was in 1895. He turned the problem over in his mind for a few days, searching for some insight that could suggest a direction to follow, but it all seemed too slippery, and his interests swung toward other things. Years later, he stumbled back onto the problem through a chance chain of events, and it took an intense and lasting hold on him. He would stubbornly hunt for a machine that he sometimes spoke of in the context of *Alice in Wonderland,* since he saw it as a chance to go roaming through the mysteries of the body. In chasing after this dream, though, he would often find himself facing scorn, apathy, ridicule, and deceit. He would become at once tortured, conquered, and exhilarated by his elusive machine.

"It was very lonely," he would say. "I was called a lunatic, a crackpot. I was the madman."

TWO

F our hundred fifty Clarkson Avenue, Brooklyn, is the address of the Downstate Medical Center, a jumble of multi-story brick towers nestled amid boxy, shade-dappled houses in one of the borough's marginal neighborhoods. Visible for blocks away, the towers draw the eye from the shabby homes. They are brutalist in style. Dim labyrinthine corridors wind through the floors, connecting the classrooms and gloomy, cramped laboratories. Institutional dourness permeates the place. Kings County Hospital, one of those brick towers, is the teaching hospital associated with Downstate, where Raymond Damadian interned.

On his arrival, Damadian was assigned to the internal medicine department. Much of the department's research at that time had to do with the fluids and electrolytes that are administered intravenously to patients. Damadian spent a good deal of his time trying to quantify the salt and water balance in the body, which demands paying considerable attention to the kidney. During the course of his internship, Damadian stashed away vast knowledge about the workings of the kidney, an organ that he found endlessly seductive, and he would talk about it to everyone, as a carpenter might enthuse about a new type of bevel.

Like any intern who hopes to advance beyond internship, he worked long and hard, sometimes twenty-four or even forty-eight hours at a stretch. He had a knack for forgetting to include a night's sleep in his routine and not missing it. When he and his wife, Donna, entertained, however, he would slowly fade until he was stretched out flat on the floor, fast asleep. "I remember waking up one night," Donna Damadian says, "because he was on his hands and knees banging on the pillow. In his dreams, someone had had cardiac arrest and he was trying to revive him. That's how intense he was about his work."

In 1961, after he completed his residency, Damadian spent a year as a postdoctoral fellow at Washington University in St. Louis with Neal Bricker, who had done research on the diseased kidney and what happens to the kidney's nephrons when it becomes impaired. The nephron is the central functioning unit of the kidney; it is a highly sophisticated filter and reabsorber. Each kidney contains some 200,000 nephrons. The function of the nephron is to excrete waste, and it must excrete it in concentrated form—as concentrated urine—in order to be efficient. So when blood from the aorta courses through the kidney, the nephrons indiscriminately squeeze out hundreds of substances, including most of the water and the sodium—the major salt in the bloodstream—and the potassium. As this filtered liquid flows farther down the nephron, a sort of evaluation process occurs. In effect, questions are asked: how's the sodium level in the body; what's the water content like; got enough potassium? Depending on the answers, varying amounts of substances get reabsorbed. Say someone has been strolling through the Sahara desert and has been finding it difficult to get a drink; the nephrons will reabsorb virtually all of the filtered water back into the bloodstream and only a few drops will be discharged as urine. Two of the important substances that get reabsorbed are sodium and potassium; they are the secret to biological electricity, which is the foundation of life. It allows us to move our arms and legs and to breathe. It's what ignites our system to get it going. Therefore, a key question for the scientist is how this absorption process takes place. Indeed, one of the central mysteries of the living cell is how it manages to concentrate certain molecules while excluding others.

One day, Damadian and some others in the lab were talking listlessly with Bricker and they asked him how the sodium is reabsorbed.

He replied, "Well, there's a sodium pump."

"Has it been isolated?" he was asked.

Bricker shook his head and said emphatically, "No. The man who does that will win the Nobel Prize."

The remark tickled Damadian's curiosity. Impossible tasks naturally appealed to him. This was the first time he had heard that the sodium pump had not yet been isolated. It was believed that the cell membrane (the outer coat) harbored "pumps" that excluded the molecules not needed for the cell's functions while pumping in those molecules that were. But no one had ever conclusively proved that these pumps existed. For all anyone knew for certain, they could be a lot of hocus-pocus. Damadian fastened onto the pump as another young man might have become smitten by the workings of the internal combustion engine. He resolved to puzzle out its secret. "At this point, I believed it existed. I had no reason not to. So, being young and full of confidence, I set out to isolate the thing."

Clearly something was going on that would suggest the existence of a pump. Cells live in a sea of salt water, which is high in sodium and low in potassium. The salt water passes through tiny, ion-sized holes in each cell at the rate of about one hundred times the volume of the cell every second. Surprisingly, the intracellular fluid—the fluid within cells—contains only 7 percent as much sodium as the salt water, but it boasts a potassium concentration that is thirty-two times greater. Since ions tend to diffuse equally into all portions of a fluid, something peculiar was keeping the body's sodium out of the cells and holding the potassium in. It made sense to many in the research community that a pump of some sort pushed excess sodium out of the cell and pulled potassium in. The pump had to have the power to shove ions into a solution that already contained too high a concentration, sort of like the brute able to cram a box of Polident and some Bermuda shorts into an already hopelessly overstuffed suitcase. Thus the pump had to possess energy. That energy was presumed to come from the molecule adenosine triphosphate, or ATP, believed to be the source for many of the energy-requiring functions of the body. Academic papers setting forth the idea of a sodium pump were published in 1941 and 1946. By the end of the decade, the concept was quite well accepted.

Bricker's lab was not the place for Damadian to grope around for the sodium pump, since it was a physiology and not a chemistry laboratory. Arthur Solomon at the department of biophysics at the Harvard Medical School, however, was doing important research on sodium metabolism. Damadian applied to work there, was quickly accepted, and migrated to Boston in 1963. He would stay for two years.

Solomon had a clever idea about how to find the pump. He suggested zeroing in on bacteria cells, which were known to pump potassium in and filter sodium out. He suggested that Damadian locate mutant bacteria with broken-down pumps or, better yet, no pumps whatsoever, and then by comparing the proteins in them to the proteins in normally functioning bacteria, he would be able to turn up the suspect protein. It sounded like a smart strategy.

Weeks and months went by in a blur as Damadian tenaciously sifted through bacteria cells, looking for mutants. His lab became a battlefield and he would sit in it, his face stern. The work proved frustratingly ineffectual until his quarry finally began to show up. "Once I found them, the hunt was on to find the pump."

In 1965, Damadian was drafted into the service. He chose

to do his two years in the Air Force and was selected to do research at the School of Aerospace Medicine at Brooks Air Force Base. Fortunately, the Air Force was interested enough in Damadian's work to allow him to continue it, as long as he also did some practical Air Force research: sifting for toxicities of hydrazine, a rocket fuel that the Air Force was using.

Day after day Damadian wore himself out looking for the elusive sodium pump. No matter what stratagem he tried, he was unable to close in on his target. The exercise was like a murder mystery without any suspects. Sometimes Damadian felt like he was working in the twilight zone. In his stomach, a sucker's empty feeling grew. "I looked and looked and looked to find this pump. I did everything that I could to try to find it. And I couldn't. To look for two years for a big strike and find nothing is discouraging. Then it occurred to me that maybe there is no pump. So I said I'd better go to the library to find out what the substantiation for this pump is. And what I found was disappointingly flimsy. Lots of sophisticated scientists wrote around the point. I traced the idea to an almost offhand suggestion by two scientists called Dean and Krogh that there might be a pump." (The names amused Damadian, for later two unrelated Washingtonians named Dean and Krogh would be implicated in the Watergate scandal.) "Everyone then seemed to pick it up. The most destructive of these were the British, who got the Nobel Prize for electricity in the nerve, who invoked the pump in their research. That made the sodium pump gospel. After that everyone believed it. The pump was actually fairly incidental to their research, but their invoking it gave it credibility."

During his pilgrimages to the library, Damadian was browsing aimlessly through the chemistry section one day when he came upon a book called *Ion Exchange*, written by Friedrich Helfferich, a German scientist then at the University of California at Berkeley. He plucked it from the shelves and started paging through it. His interest was arrested. He took the book home and read every word of it. "Somebody in my field would never have read that book. I think if you looked at all the people doing sodium-pump work, and there are thousands, I bet not one read that book." That would not be startling. The book, after all, was about chemistry, not biology, and had nothing at all to do with medicine. "But I read this book and I said this is it. This is what the cell is doing."

Recalling the episode, Damadian seems to re-create his enthusiasm of that distant moment. "It was dynamite. I can't explain what this book meant to me. I could have looked for the rest of my life for the sodium pump and never found it. This book told me to stop looking."

Ion exchange, as the book pointed out, is ubiquitous in nature. Granites do it. Clays do it. Plants do it. Animals do it. Damadian especially liked a passage by the author in the book's introduction that suggested that ion exchange could be traced all the way back to Biblical times and quoted a passage from Exodus recounting the actions of Moses: "They could not drink of the waters of Marah, for they were bitter; and Jehovah showed him a tree, and he cast it into the waters, and the waters were made sweet." As Helfferich wrote: "Thus Moses succeeded in preparing drinking water from brackish water, undoubtedly by an ion-exchange technique which he developed on an industrial scale. About a thousand years later, Aristotle stated that seawater loses part of its salt content when percolating through certain sands."

A simple way to understand ion exchange, and one cited in the book, is in terms of its most common application—the water softener. The water softener, in essence, is an ion exchanger. A lot of people have water that is full of calcium and zinc, making it undesirable for cooking and bathing. So they get a water softener. Inside it is a substance called vinyl benzene that forms into beads. The beads are negatively charged by negative sulfonate groups impregnating them. Calcium has two plus charges on it, as does zinc. You set up the beads with sodium attached to the negative charges of the beads; sodium is positive and has one plus charge. Then when the water with the calcium comes through, the double plus of the calcium has a stronger affinity for the negatively charged sulfonate on the bead than does the single plus of the sodium. So the sodium is exchanged for calcium and the water emerges from the softener with sodium rather than calcium. The same thing happens with the zinc. It turns out that if you study this bead carefully, you will find it has a greater affinity for some substances over others. You can thus draw up a chart, and no two substances on it will be precisely equal in their affinity.

Damadian also encountered another book in the library that he had heard about years ago but had never bothered to read because his colleagues derided its author as a "kook." The book, published in 1962, was *A Physical Theory of the Living State* by a Chinese-American physiologist named Gilbert Ling. "He claimed there was no sodium pump, which took enormous courage, enormous courage," Damadian says. "I still can't believe he did it. In fact, I doubt that I would have had the courage to say that. I would now, but probably not then. To declare that all these people who had won Nobel Prizes were wrong! That's tantamount to saying that the sun didn't rise in the morning."

Ling believed that the conventionally accepted model of living forces in the human cell was wrongheaded. The cell was basically looked on as a bag of water with proteins dissolved in the solution. Ling felt, instead, that water in cells is not free-flowing but exists in multiple layers of water molecules, which Ling called multiple polarized layers. Cell water, Ling believed, was much less fluid than free water. He suggested that there are negative charges within the cell that are anchored to its insides and can't shake loose. Thus potassium, being positively charged, is held inside almost as if by magnetism. And that is how the cell accumulates all these ions. He did not believe, however, that the cell was an ion-exchange resin. Damadian thought it was. Ling dismissed that idea, Damadian thinks, because it seemed too simple for something "as majestic as the cell."

A common research tool used by Ling and others was frog muscle. If you took the muscle of a frog and clamped it between two plastic chambers and then filled the chambers with water and chemicals, the muscle would pump sodium in just one direction. Ling, in one experiment, calculated how much energy was necessary to run a sodium pump. Then he calculated how much energy was generated by the frog muscle. He concluded that there wasn't nearly enough energy to operate any such pump, that a pump operating at 100 percent efficiency would need at least fifteen to thirty times as much energy as was available, and thus the notion was a complete fraud. The rest of the scientific community, except for a small band of Ling disciples, either ridiculed him as a madman or simply ignored him altogether. For him to be right, a long list of scientific theories would have to be discarded.

But Damadian was willing to believe, and he resolved to undertake his own investigations to see if Ling was right. "I was not prepared to accept anything at this point without validating it myself. I had no interest in running the risk of heading off on another wild goose chase."

Discharged from the Air Force in 1967, Damadian weighed a number of offers from various universities where he could have carried on his cell research and finally chose to return to Downstate and join the biophysical laboratory of the department of medicine. Part of his motivation was to help build a more innovative internal medicine department with a strong basis in the biophysics area.

A MACHINE CALLED INDOMITABLE

The man who recruited Damadian was Ludwig Eichna. He was an unusual person with unusual aspirations. Scrupulous, fair-minded, serious almost to a fault, Eichna had enormous tolerance for the unorthodox. Years later, upon his retirement from Downstate, he would enroll in medical school for a second time, going through its rigors with students decades younger, for the purpose of writing a book comparing the experience of a greenhorn student with that of a seasoned educator. He was a student of many professors who had once been his own students. As chairman of the internal medicine department, Eichna wished to transform doctors into scientists. Research for the sake of research was a high priority. "Eichna dreamed of the day when chemists and biophysicists could go to the bedside of patients and address problems in terms of physics and chemistry," Damadian says. "In the past, it had been bread-and-butter types with stethoscopes." Damadian decided to return to Downstate largely because of Eichna's support, which he knew would be essential if he embarked on disproving a concept as firmly entrenched as the sodium pump. "A scientist, particularly a daring one, needs that. Because everyone is always trying to silence you."

Damadian was assigned a tiny laboratory on the sixth floor of the biophysics building. It was a small, dank, desultorily furnished space, the floors of well-worn linoleum tile. The desks and shelves were quickly overloaded with papers and files and flasks. Order was not always evident or even in existence. Hardly ever was anything dusted, sorted, or put away in its proper place. Colleagues would lend journals to Damadian only to have them disappear into the chaos of the lab. Damadian would forget he had ever seen them. A search party would be necessary to find them.

In his new position, Damadian began in earnest to try to corroborate what he now saw shaping up as a new theory of life. It was a heady experience for him. As he would often tell

15

others, "I always wanted to do something very, very important. I think it has to do with vision and imagination, what kind of goals you set for yourself. Someone with a lot of vision may say, 'I want to jump to the moon.' Someone without imagination won't even imagine jumping to the moon. I was a dreamer. It was a curse, in a sense. The frustration of not being able to realize those dreams is very powerful."

Gregarious and outspoken—hardly the stereotypical scientist who slips into his lab, starts mixing fluids in flasks, and never more than grunts to any interloper—Damadian immediately became a visible and idiosyncratic presence. Anyone who passed within striking distance of the lab would find himself buttonholed and engaged in conversation that might continue for an hour if not a week. Damadian liked a virile give-and-take atmosphere. He was hardly bashful about presenting himself as the prickly outsider. He would deliver sermons on ion exchange, his new concept of the cell, topics that to most of his listeners seemed utterly bizarre, from somewhere in the science-fiction future. One colleague, after quizzically listening to a few of Damadian's soliloquies, would remember thinking to himself: "Well, we've got a live one!"

Damadian shortly afterward hired a heavyset young man named Michael Goldsmith to assist him, and they began to experiment with potassium and sodium. "We were finding that water controlled the choice of potassium over sodium," Damadian said. "The amount of water inside the cell and its structure were the dominant factors that controlled the cell's selectivity for these ions. Anytime we messed with the water that the bugs were suspended in, by putting in agents such as sugars or salts, we could increase or decrease the affinity for potassium. If we put a lot of inert sugar into the water, the ratio of potassium to sodium changed. If the sugar particles can't get into the cell, then they pull water out of the cell to dissolve them by a process called osmosis. By putting in other agents, such that water was added to the cell, then a change in the balance would occur again."

Soon another student, Larry Minkoff, joined Damadian's lab, and the two of them did a study of the energy contained in the cell, determining that the cell was able to muster only about 14 percent of the energy necessary to run a pump. The results were written up in a paper titled "Caloric Catastrophe," which ruffled a lot of important feathers. In it, Damadian and Minkoff concluded, "On the basis of the measurements and calculations in this paper, we find membrane models of solute transport dependent on ATP for energy to be thermodynamically untenable. We therefore conclude that the present pump models as constituted pose a serious dilemma, a caloric catastrophe." The paper did a lot to convince the mainstream scientific community that a harebrained individual had come onto the scene.

It was not long after his arrival at Downstate that Damadian began to formulate his own theory of the cell. Like Ling, he felt that it was the way in which the cell's contents were organized that governed the coming and going of molecules. He believed that the contents of the cell were organized into a systematic molecular structure, with the molecules being held in place by electric charges on atoms. He explains, "The cell may be regarded as an ion-exchange resin bead with respect to the way it takes in and expels molecules, much like the ion-exchange resin beads that take up and expel molecules in the commercial ion exchangers that soften water for household use." If an atom fits into this structure, then the cell holds it. If it doesn't fit, then it passes out of the cell.

Central to his theory was a substance so ubiquitous that most previous researchers had discounted its importance. That substance was water. A charged particle is water-loving, and thus a charged particle will never be naked; it will always go around with a water covering. Since water is dipole, when you drop a molecule like potassium or sodium into it, the tendency is for the water to cluster around it. Potassium and sodium are the dominant members of the alkali metals group in physiology. The bigger molecules attract less water than smaller ones, because the smaller ones have a greater density of charge. So smaller molecules in a hydrated state need the most water. Thus, in terms of selectivity, if a cell has a limit as to how much water it can hold (which it does), then it will choose the ions that are the most sparing in terms of how much water they require. Potassium is a larger molecule than sodium. If the two choices confronting a cell are sodium and potassium, the cell will choose potassium over sodium.

When cells die, they relax and also fill up with water. Why is it, Damadian wondered, that cells have limits to how much water they can hold? Eventually, he reasoned, there must be a controlling mechanism in the cell that regulates its volume. He concluded it was metabolism. He believed there was a tonus, which he called cynotonus, that was the arbiter of the volume of the cell.

Jubilant and enormously excited about this concept, Damadian, in one of those leaps his mind habitually made, began to think of how the theory could be applied to disease. It had been observed by previous researchers that when a normal cell is transformed into a wild-growing cancerous cell, the internal organization of the cell collapses, as the interior walls and floors of a house do when a fire erupts. The cancer cell becomes a sloppy mess. It fills up with water. It can't distinguish between sodium and potassium, or distinguish anything at all for that matter. Therefore, it seemed likely to Damadian that it would be possible to detect the difference between a cancerous cell and a normal cell purely from its chemistry, rather than from its appearance under a microscope. Among other things, cancer cells were known to contain elevated levels of potassium. From his experiments and his theory, Damadian felt that the reason for that variation was a change in the water structure—that is, in the multiple polarized layers of water molecules that Gilbert Ling and practically no one else believed cells contained. In Damadian's head, this all made perfect sense. At this juncture, though, it was still no more than conjecture that was far from being established with anything like rocklike certainty.

THREE

W ELCOME BIOLOGISTS was the message on the billboards, and it was duly noted by the procession of cars filing into the city. Welcome they should be. The biologists would occupy virtually every hotel room, fill up all the tables in the restaurants. It was April 1969 in Atlantic City, New Jersey. It was cold, spitty weather—a fact of little significance to the members of the Federation of American Societies of Experimental Biology, who had converged on this seaside resort for the group's annual convention. Damadian was one of the hundreds who drove past the welcoming signs. He was looking forward to the convocation, since it offered an opportunity to discuss his current work with fellow researchers, to swap thoughts and gossip. And indeed, once he got there, he bumped into Gilbert Ling, with whom he had been communicating for the last couple of years.

One evening, Damadian joined his Philadelphia friend for a leisurely conversational dinner at Zaberer's restaurant. Ling also invited along a physiologist named Carlton Hazlewood and a physicist-physician named Freeman Cope. Both Hazlewood and Cope were devout disciples of Ling. Cope, in fact, came to be known as the prophet of the structured-water advocates, tirelessly trumpeting the theory and its implications to the disbelieving medical community. Hazlewood was on the faculty of the Baylor College of Medicine in Houston and was working on a basic problem of muscle development. A huge, powerfully built man, he had picked up badly needed spending money when he was a graduate student by moonlighting as a professional wrestler. Damadian found him eminently likable, but he was particularly taken by the peppy, genially dignified Cope.

Then thirty-eight, Cope traced his ancestors to the New England Puritans. He was the grandson of Edward Lee Thorndike, the educator and lexicographer. Cope possessed an enormous intellect. He could read more than two thousand words a minute. He lived alone in a four-room second-story apartment in Doylestown, Pennsylvania. He slept in one room and used the other three to house his staggering collection of books. His landlord often feared that the floor one day would give way under the daunting weight of all the volumes. Damadian came to know Cope much better in subsequent months and years and concluded that Cope was unquestionably the most honest man he had ever met. "He was very intense, but a pleasant, compassionate human being. I got the idea that besides research and reading the only other thing he did was talk to me on the telephone for hours and hours. He was incredibly honest. Most people when squeezed will bend the facts. But Cope never lied. He was constantly caught in situations that were contrary to his welfare, but he wouldn't lie. About the worst thing he would do is stare at you and say nothing."

At the time, Cope was doing research in the biological division of the United States Naval Air Development Center in Warminster, Pennsylvania. His main interest was seeing whether electricity is conducted in biological systems the same way it is in a transistor. Cope had just measured sodium in the brain and kidney, using a device known as a nuclear magnetic resonance (NMR) spectrometer, and had determined that it was more like a solid than a liquid. This finding had made something of a splash. Cope was hoping next to attack potassium, though it had a much fainter signal for the spectrometer to detect. Hardly anything, though, frightened him; he was completely at ease dancing around on the lips of the unknown. He had persuaded the Nuclear Magnetic Resonance Specialties Corporation, a small manufacturer in New Kensington, Pennsylvania, on the outskirts of Pittsburgh, to let him use its powerful magnet. It was a cylindrical device about eighteen inches in diameter and four and a half feet tall. The center of the cylinder was a hollow vertical bore into which operators of the spectrometer could place samples. The president of NMR Specialties, a kindly man named Paul Yajko, was pleased to oblige scientists, since, after all, they were his customers.

Damadian's eyes stayed on Cope as he explained his work in crisp sentences over the dinner table at Zaberer's. Cope was worried that his next experiment might fail, because living cells simply didn't have enough potassium to give off an NMR signal. When it became possible to get a word in (the trick was to time things so that your mouth was empty when Cope took a forkful), Damadian told Cope he believed he might be able to help. He said he probably could get his hands on some bacteria from the Dead Sea that had twenty times the normal potassium content.

Two weeks later, Cope called Damadian asking for the stuff. Damadian delivered on his promise, and soon afterward they were driving their cars together on the Pennsylvania Turnpike, Cope with his Volkswagen choked with electronic gear and Damadian with his car jammed with culture media and assorted bacteria-growing equipment, heading for NMR Specialties. They stopped at turnpike restaurants and fell into intense discussions. At the first stop, Damadian, absorbed in debate, locked his car doors with his keys still in the ignition. A garage mechanic, after great effort, managed to unlatch one door with a coat hanger. Damadian, still engrossed in the debate, thanked him, pushed down the button, and closed the door, the keys still dangling inside. The stunned Cope began to wonder what sort of fellow he had befriended. When the two finally reached their destination, they checked into a Holiday Inn near the company and, expectations rising though still in check, went off to do their experiments.

Nuclear magnetic resonance was discovered in the 1940s by two physicists, Edward M. Purcell of Harvard University and Felix Bloch of Stanford University, an achievement that won them the Nobel Prize in 1952. Working unbeknownst to each other, the two men came to their brilliant discoveries almost simultaneously and published their results in 1946 in consecutive issues of the journal *Physical Review*. The phenomenon they identified results from the fact that atoms whose nuclei boast an odd number of protons or neutrons (most atoms do) continually spin like little tops and behave like miniature bar magnets of the sort you might use to fasten shopping reminders to the refrigerator door. In a normal state, these spinning atoms are randomly oriented. When they are exposed to an external magnetic field, however, the field acts on the nuclei's magnetic poles and tries to line them up as they spin. This alignment force causes them to precess, or wobble like a gyrating top, and eventually to line up, according to the standard analogy, much like soldiers on parade. The soldiers actually divide into two platoons—a lower, more populous energy group whose spins line up with the direction of the magnetic field, and a higher-energy platoon in which the nuclear magnets oppose the magnet's field. If a radio wave, not any different from the signal that might originate from a radio station, is beamed at right angles to the magnetic field, the wobbling nuclei in the lower platoon absorb the energy, resonate and do a quarter turn, and make a "spin flip" or jump to the upper platoon.

Each of these tiny magnets wobbles at its own particular frequency. This is called its resonant frequency (or Larmor frequency), and it depends on the magnetism of the nucleus and the strength of the magnetic field. The difference in this frequency between two atoms in the body has been characterized as being twenty to forty times farther apart than the FM stations on your stereo tuner (typically half a megahertz apart), and thus it becomes possible, in effect, to tune in your favorite atom the way you tune in your favorite radio station. In order for an atom to be boosted into the higher-energy group, the radio wave's frequency must match that of the nucleus's natural spin—hence the term "nuclear magnetic resonance." It is similar to what would happen if you took a tuning fork for the musical note A and set it vibrating, then brought a second tuning fork for the note A alongside the first. The second fork would start vibrating as well. This phenomenon is called resonance. A tuning fork for the note C wouldn't vibrate when brought alongside the A fork because it wouldn't be in resonance.

Once the soldiers have reached the upper platoon, if the radio pulse is switched off, they will slowly realign themselves with the magnetic field and tumble back to the lower group. When they tumble back, the nuclei emit the energy that they have absorbed. The magnitude of the energy is directly related to the density of the nuclei in a region, and thus the signal generated by it becomes a telltale fingerprint that can be measured to characterize the nuclei. Since the resonance frequency of a particular nucleus in one environment differs from the frequency of the same nucleus in a different environment, the nuclear signal can be used to report what the atom's neighbors are. With the aid of a radio receiver and an antenna wrapped around the sample, these faint currents can be detected and then monitored on an oscilloscope. The amount of time for the nuclei to return to equilibrium (their so-called relaxation times) can also be measured in two distinct ways to further describe the atom's character. These are referred to as T1 and T2. T1, or spin-lattice relaxation, characterizes the interaction between a nucleus and the environment (lattice). T2, or spin-spin relaxation, describes the interaction between a nucleus and surrounding nuclei. These speeds fluctuate depending on the physical environment of the nucleus, in the way that a swimmer would take longer to forge his way through choppy water than through a calm sea.

What was the practical payout of NMR? Almost at once, it became a prized tool among organic chemists, who used the technique to dope out the composition of single compounds in pure solutions. Among the topics for which NMR furnished detailed information were the structure of molecules, chemical bonding, crystal structure, reaction rates and chemical equilibrium, and internal motions in solids and liquids. The technique also became useful, as more powerful magnets were applied, to view the coordinated chemical activity of cells. A small number of chemists began to experiment with biological applications. In fact, soon after making his discovery Bloch poked his finger into the coil of his spectrometer and got an NMR signal. In 1948, Purcell and a fellow scientist wrapped their heads with a coil attached to a radio frequency generator and then stuck them in the field of the Harvard cyclotron. The only thing they sensed as they shoved their heads in and out of the magnet was the magnetic field that was generated in the metal fillings of their teeth.

The nucleus of most interest in biological studies was the hydrogen proton, since it emits a relatively strong signal and is by far the most abundant nucleus in living tissue. The chemists' machines were mostly tiny things that used a steady but powerful magnetic field and detected one signal from the entire sample, which had to be small enough to fit inside a test tube. The test tube would be placed between poles of a magnet, and a radio frequency field would be generated by a coil encircling the sample. The energy would then be displayed on a spectrometer. No information about the relative location of the resonating nuclei, however, could be determined from conventional NMR signals. Consequently, they were useless in examining the constantly changing structures of complex, living tissues.

Damadian had in fact been introduced fleetingly to NMR by one of its pioneers. While he was at Harvard in 1963, he took a course entitled Introduction to Quantum Mechanics, given by Edward Purcell. One day, as part of some now-forgotten discussion, Purcell drew an NMR spectrum on the board. Intrigued, Damadian recognized that such a device might be helpful in the sodium-pump work he was doing in Solomon's lab, though he wasn't sure exactly how it might be useful. Damadian approached Solomon later in the day and asked him if they could use nuclear magnetic resonance—he didn't actually know it was called that at the time—and Solomon said that he was sorry but the machines were too expensive.

At NMR Specialties, Damadian watched with taut attentiveness as Cope inserted several samples into the NMR machine and obtained signals on an oscilloscope. He did not fully understand Cope's manipulations of the machine, but he knew beyond question what he was seeing when the signals began to show up. He felt something like a blind man who had just been given sight. "I remember the first time I saw a potassium signal," he would say many years later. "This huge blip filled the oscilloscope screen. I had never seen an NMR machine, and it had a profound effect on me. I mean, wow! In a few seconds we were taking a measurement that would usually take me weeks and sometimes months to do accurately. I had a reaction to the potency of this. It was doing chemistry by wireless electronics."

Damadian and Cope spent two busy weeks in New Kensington. After a morning of glimpsing NMR signals at NMR

Specialties, they would reconnoiter for lunch back at the Holiday Inn. The dining room and its oak tables looked out upon the lawn-framed swimming pool, and, when there was not a spray of dialogue, they would often gaze out at the pool, the sunlight angling through the large windows and spilling into the restaurant. They would lose themselves in thought and wonder about the blips they had observed that day.

One afternoon, peering at the pool (as he has later recounted the story), Damadian went off into his own mind. Gradually, swirling like smoke, visions emerged. Perhaps some sort of giant NMR machine might be just the device that could be used to scan his stomach (which was still acting up) and get at what really ailed him. He was convinced, because of the research work that he was doing, that the composition of a cancer cell had to be different from that of a normal cell. He knew that the proportion of sodium to potassium ions was not the same in a cancer cell, and so, according to his ion-exchange theory, the water structure had to be different. The water was the key thing, because the hydrogen in water boasted the strongest NMR signal. If cancer cells indeed had different water structures than normal cells, then NMR signals from protons of water ought to be discernibly different in cancerous tissue than in normal tissue. If that was true, then why couldn't he develop an NMR scanner to probe the human body for cancer? Open a new window into life?

Damadian shared his thoughts with Cope. Let's pursue this together, he urged him. His luncheon partner heard all this talk amiably. As they conversed, though, a frown formed on Cope's face. He was gravely dubious. Rummaging through his mind, he catalogued the hurdles involved. It would take years—probably a decade—to convince people of the possibility. The opposing forces would be brutal and unremitting. It would take years just to perform the experiments and design the powerful equipment that could make scanning the body a reality. The cost would be monstrous; finding the necessary funding would not be easy. No, Cope said, it was just too heroic an undertaking. Try something else.

Damadian tactfully changed the subject. Cope's doubtful attitude was not at all surprising. As Damadian would later point out, "You have to understand that we were talking about machines then that were wide enough to take something no bigger than a pencil. What I was talking about was like going from a paper glider that you tossed across the classroom to a 747."

Damadian harbored extremely mixed feelings about the prospect of pursuing his idea. Sober, cautious thoughts assailed him. After all, he was deep into his own ion-exchange research. He felt it was profoundly important. Was he ready to put that aside to work on something so speculative? Science, he well knew, moves in fits and starts. Thousands of ideas flutter through a scientist's mind, but only a few are truly significant. Even fewer actually work. It is often all but impossible to predict whether an idea is worth pursuing. "When it occurred to me, I thought it was a fool thing to do. I had spent ten years doing one thing, and here I was thinking about going off on some tangent. It's like you're going down the main drag on the path of your life, pretty happy about how things are going, you know, no real complaints, and you suddenly take a hard right and head off on some dirt road. It made no sense to do it. I mean, why leave the highway?"

The potassium experiments went well, which pleased Damadian. What continued to gnaw away at him, though, was the hope that he could use some derivative of this wondrous machine to scan patients for cancer. Put medicine on the road to a new rainbow. Cope's lack of encouragement notwithstanding, Damadian could not let the impulse go. Before leaving New Kensington, he cornered Paul Yajko and asked him if it would be all right if he returned sometime soon to try a few more experiments on one of his NMR machines. It wouldn't take terribly long. Yajko said yes, that would be just fine.

Once he returned to Downstate, Damadian told Goldsmith and Minkoff all about his ideas. He would share his notions with them and hone them against their common sense. In their youthful vigor, they, too, were absorbed by the possibilities and thought the conception certainly ought to be pursued.

In June 1970, taking the dirt road as it were, Damadian trekked alone to New Kensington, the trunk of his car crammed with cages containing six rats implanted with tumors of Walker sarcoma, a strain of cancer that grows easily and rapidly in rats. He got a room at the Holiday Inn and drove over to NMR Specialties. He was shown to a machine, handed a sketchy operator's manual, and told that unfortunately there was no one free to explain how to work it. Several days passed before he had even mastered the machine well enough to begin his experiments.

"I said, let's see if I can distinguish diseased tissue from normal tissue. I took the rats with tumors and cut out tumor samples. I put a tumor sample in a test tube and measured the relaxation time. Then I cut some normal tissue from some rats and measured that to see if the relaxation time was different. To my amazement, it wasn't just different, it was considerably different. The tumorous samples had longer relaxation times, which squared with my theory. Okay, this was great, this was terrific. But I had a problem. The problem was were the numbers really different or had I screwed up because I was such a novice? I ran more and more tissue. The results were the same. I could now distinguish cancerous tissue from normal tissue by the NMR signal. No one had ever suggested this before, and I just knew I could do this on the whole human body."

Having exhausted his supply of rats, Damadian departed

New Kensington after a week, guardedly excited. "I was a novice," he says. "I was all alone. Nobody had ever done this before. I certainly wasn't unconscious of the magnitude of the discovery. At the same time, I was anxious about reporting something of this magnitude. I knew it would attract a lot of attention. If you're wrong, it's more than a little bit embarrassing. It's very, very embarrassing."

He resolved to run further tests, and so, three weeks later, in the first week of July, he returned to New Kensington, checked in once again at the Holiday Inn, and went over with his fresh supply of rats to NMR Specialties. He decided that after this much time away from the machine, if he could return to it with new rats, start up the device again from scratch, and redo the measurements still as a novice operator, then the findings must be real. He had rats with two types of tumors this time, Walker sarcoma and Novikoff hepatoma, to make sure his findings were not a quirk of one strain of cancer. He stayed a full week and accumulated both T1 and T2 readings from the kidney, muscle, stomach, intestine, brain, and liver. In each instance, there were noticeable differences in the relaxation times between cancerous and healthy tissues. To take some examples, the T1 relaxation time for protons in water molecules in normal rat liver tissue was 0.293 second, while the Novikoff hepatoma samples produced a time of 0.826 second and the Walker sarcoma was 0.736 second.

In the Holiday Inn lunchroom, overlooking the swimming pool, Damadian began to work on a paper to report his findings, scribbling in one of his spiral notebooks. The view of the pool kept catching his eye. A calvacade of visions glided through his mind—big, sleek machines, people being scanned by them, disease being detected. "Now I was really excited. There's a big difference in the psychology of planning to do something and the psychology of actually doing it and seeing the result. I had discovered the scanning signal, the diseased signal that would report the presence and location of cancer in the body to the scanner."

At once, Damadian saw far-reaching possibilities for NMR in medicine. He pictured it as a way to diagnose the severity of a disease by using numbers. He imagined assigning numbers, sort of like batting averages, to a disease. He saw it moving medicine from qualitative to quantitative science. He also realized that NMR had applications far beyond cancer. "Once I made the hit with cancer, it was immediately obvious to me that it would be good for all diseases—for heart disease, kidney disease, mental disease, the works."

One of the people Damadian conveyed pieces of his vision to was Donald Vickers, a wry, easygoing fellow who was in charge of finding applications for the machines that NMR Specialties made. "I remember him very excitedly telling me about putting people in NMR machines," Vickers says. "I don't know if he totally knew what he wanted to do when he put them in there, but he definitely wanted to put them in there. And the man was definitely pumped up. The fellow was flying."

Damadian finished polishing his paper soon after his return to Downstate and promptly submitted it to his department chairman, Ludwig Eichna, as well as to *Science* magazine. Eichna didn't like the paper. He thought the language in it was too daring and ordered Damadian to tone it down. Damadian did as instructed, and *Science* published it in its issue of March 19, 1971, under the title "Tumor Detection by Nuclear Magnetic Resonance." The paper began, "At present, early detection of internal neoplasms is hampered by the relatively high permeability of many tumors to X-rays. In principle, nuclear magnetic resonance (NMR) techniques combine many of the desirable features of an external probe for the detection of internal cancer." The paper went on to talk about the radical water-structure theory and its role in explaining the biological changes that brought about the elevated relaxation times in the cancerous samples.

Even in its toned-down form, it was a brassy paper. "It's always tricky when to publish in science," Damadian says. "You can wait too long and do too many tests and you can get scooped. If you publish too quickly, you can be wrong. This was a big thing. It was like a gold strike, and I didn't want to wait until I registered my claim."

At the same time, he knew that his assertions were so audacious that most members of the scientific community were likely to look askance at him. As he has since remarked, "A really important part of doing something new is putting your reputation on the line and taking the brickbats that come with it. I said it back in 1971, and I knew I was going to be perceived as a screaming lunatic. But I felt that it had to be done. Maybe I feared the final irony of sitting by while somebody in my family got the rotten disease."

Considerable excitement was indeed stirred up by the *Science* paper, and many researchers around the country sniffed at its conclusions and hurriedly began their own work to repeat and verify Damadian's claims. It was a particularly timely discovery, because President Nixon, through the passage of the National Cancer Act, had declared his intention to spend a billion dollars a year to try once and for all to slay cancer. Stanley Goldstein, an associate professor of pediatrics at Downstate, heard about Damadian's ideas and remembers thinking, "This man is onto something big. I thought he was a brilliant man. I thought he might be a genius. I thought this was *Star Wars*. To me, this was Buck Rogers and Flash Gordon."

The paper also drew a good measure of derision, largely because of the grand claims Damadian had made and because of his belief in the structured-water theory of the cell. Damadian was already in a maverick camp when he came into NMR out of left field. His cell theory alone was enough for many scientists to brand him a crackpot. If he believed that, well, then what didn't he believe? As Don Vickers would recall: "He provoked quite a few chuckles in the staid NMR community. As far as it was concerned, NMR was for high-resolution samples, and putting people in there was ridiculous."

Damadian, however, adored the idea. It was just the sort of grand notion that he had always wanted to fasten onto, and he was ready to bet his career that it would amount to something. Anxious to press on and undertake NMR investigations of human tissue, he ordered his own NMR machine for his Downstate lab. "Raymond would say to me, 'Once you get an idea it's not controllable,'" Vickers says. "'Once you have an idea in your head, you can't not use it. It's like if you're in a hole trying to get out and you have the idea to climb a rope and there's a rope dangling in the hole. It's not reasonable to say, "I'm going to come up with some other way to get out of this hole.' You're going to climb that rope. So Damadian climbed the rope."

In the spring of 1971, the public relations department at Downstate wanted to do a story on Damadian for the campus publication. Ed Edelson, a free-lance science writer, was retained to write the piece. The article, published in the spring 1971 edition of the *Downstate Reporter*, started out, "Sometime in June, a truck will pull up at Downstate bearing a 14-foot-high machine for the biophysics laboratory of Dr. Raymond Damadian, Assistant Professor of Medicine and of Biophysics.

"The machine is a nuclear magnetic resonance instrument, which is more at home in physics or chemistry laboratories than in medical institutions. But to Dr. Damadian, the device is very much a medical instrument. He regards it as the prototype of a machine-to-be that could fulfill a longstanding dream of physicians: a quick, foolproof method of early cancer detection.

"Already, Dr. Damadian is planning to build a much larger nuclear magnetic resonance device, one that will be big enough to hold a human being. That machine, Dr. Damadian believes, will prove that nuclear magnetic resonance (NMR) is the tool that doctors have been looking for in their quest for a method of detecting cancer early, when treatment is most effective. . . ."

After recounting some of Damadian's background and the work that had led him to this juncture, Edelson, in the twenty-first paragraph of the story, wrote: "The proposed NMR device for detecting cancer in humans would not have to be highly elaborate, Dr. Damadian says. It would consist of a large coil to emit radio waves and a movable magnet to create the magnetic field required. The coil would be wrapped around the patient's chest, while the magnet passed back and forth across the body. A detector would pick up NMR emissions for analysis."

When discussing the article some years later, Damadian explained, "When he was doing the story, he said, 'Raymond, I don't understand how this is going to work.' He said, 'Okay, you get a signal from a test tube, but how are you going to do it in a body with all that other tissue present?' I said, 'That's easy. I'm going to lay the person down and move the magnet back and forth across him. The selected signal-producing region within the magnet will provide the needed spatial localization.' That was the first time that a method was published to produce the volume localization needed for scanning the body by NMR."

Spatial localization was a critical concept, for without it there could be no human scanning. Similar signals from different parts of the body would overlap and create a useless mass. How, for instance, was one to tell if NMR signals from atoms in the head were coming from the brain or from the tongue? Damadian likens the focusing problem to the dilemma faced by an orbiting satellite that picks up radio signals from all over the earth but is interested only in what is being sent from Toledo.

The focusing technique Damadian thought up, which he eventually named FONAR (an alternating acronym that stands for "field focused nuclear magnetic resonance"), works by shaping the magnetic field across the entire sample so as to construct a small resonant window at the particular point of interest. His idea was to use a magnet that produced a saddle-shaped field. Such a magnet boasts markedly different field strengths along its sloping surface. The radio frequency that would be used to excite the wobbling nuclei would correspond to the field strength at the nadir or "saddle point" of the magnet. Hence, NMR signals would be detected only from this point. Nuclei in other parts of the sample would either be resonating at a different frequency or would be situated in areas where the field strength was so steeply graded that too little signal would be generated to be detected.

Until questioned about the focusing problem by Edelson, Damadian had not given it any particular thought. "I had just figured that I could get the cancer signal out of there. I didn't know how I would do it, but I figured it was an abnormal signal and I would get it out somehow. Not until Edelson pinned me down on it did I think it through and figure it out. I did it in maybe a minute. I did know that in a regular NMR machine there was a single point in the magnet which would produce a signal. I knew that there was a specific location that was important. I didn't know it was called the saddle point or anything. I didn't know any of the words. When I thought of how to do it while talking with Edelson, I was quite proud of myself."

Having worked this focusing idea out, Damadian prepared a patent application for a scanning device to detect cancer that he eventually filed on March 17, 1972.

Around this time, a public company in Texas called Hycel Electronics, which made blood analyzers, became aware of Damadian's work through some newspaper coverage that his discovery attracted. Hycel was, in particular, intrigued by a story in a Houston newspaper that characterized Damadian as the modern-day "Bones" McCoy, the physician on *Star Trek*. When a crew member contracted some uncertain ailment, Dr. McCoy would scan him with a futuristic machine (exactly how it worked was never made clear) that would instantly reveal the source of the problem: tumors perhaps, or edema, or maybe chemical changes in the brain. McCoy would then whip up a cure in the spaceship's lab. Imagining that they had a chance to hire the real-life Dr. McCoy, Hycel officials contacted Damadian about obtaining the rights to his research.

In April 1971, Damadian prepared a six-page summary of what he hoped to do and what it would cost. It was typical Damadian: visionary, bold, immodest. He talked about beginning "construction of an NMR detector that can be used to hunt down cancers in humans." He went on, "Such detectors would constitute standard equipment in hospitals, clinics, and doctors' offices. Patients would be scanned twice annually, for example, as a routine part of medical practice, to systematize the program of early cancer detection. . . . In a practical sense, the development of this instrument is regarded as the single greatest chance for the obliteration of cancer. Its success does not rest on the indefinite hope of finding the 'cause' of cancer but is a practical strategy depending only on our capacity to apply existing technology, a technology capable of putting a man on the moon. Furthermore, it is understood that the applications of this detector will not be limited to cancer but will have use whenever chemical information is sought directly from tissues and organs within the human body. In effect, to the extent that medical practice becomes molecular medicine, it will replace X-ray equipment since it will provide chemical anatomy in place of the pictorial anatomy now provided by X-rays."

Damadian went on to estimate that it would take him at most three years, and probably a much shorter period, to build the first human detector. Initial equipment expenses, he roughly estimated, would total four hundred and fifty thousand dollars. Another ninety-one thousand dollars per year would be needed for salaries, including thirty thousand dollars for Damadian himself, the same income he was currently drawing from Downstate. In a general sense, Hycel agreed to the stipulations, and contract preparations were set in motion. Negotiations on the fine points, however, would eventually plod on for more than a year. During the course of the interminable discussions, the company sent a cell biologist and a physical chemist to New York to peruse Damadian's work and listen to his explanations. They decided it was impossible to build a human scanner and advised the company not to invest in such a foolhardy venture. Hycel's interest continued nonetheless, but the contract terms, from Damadian's perspective, grew more and more prohibitive. For instance, Hycel attached a clause that specified that if Damadian invented anything, whatever it might be, Hycel would own the rights to it. As Damadian put it, "So if I invented a lawnmower, that would be theirs. If I came up with a new spot remover, they'd get it." The sum of money originally agreed upon shrank. Damadian refused to sign the contract, and Hycel didn't press him. Much later, Damadian told himself, they would mightily regret their decision.

FOUR

When Raymond Damadian was a young man, growing up in a working-class Queens neighborhood, he had three overriding passions—science, the violin, and tennis. He shone at all of them. By any of a number of twists of fate, it is entirely possible that he could now be a member of the New York Philharmonic or a retired veteran—Wimbledon cups to reminisce with—of the tennis wars. He also toyed seriously with the idea of becoming a medical missionary, trooping through foreign jungles to heal the sick.

Damadian's childhood was presided over by an adoring father and a disciplinarian mother. Damadian's mother, Odette Yazedjian, was the daughter of a French mother and an Armenian father. Her father, Haig Yazedjian, came to the United States from France in 1906, settling in New York, where he was the country's first distributor of Renault cars. He also raced the cars professionally but gave up the sport under stiff marital pressure when Odette was born. That will be all with your crazy racing, his wife more or less told him, you're a family man now. A few years later, he opened a livery to ferry the well-heeled around town. The fleet consisted of three Renault limousines. The backseat of each was always decorated with a crystal vase containing fresh roses; when the weather turned sharp, fur blankets were available to snuggle under. Yazedjian was too kindhearted to be a successful businessman. If a customer didn't pay his bills, Yazedjian made little effort to collect. His most renowned customer, and a steady non-bill-payer, was Enrico Caruso. To compensate for all the unpaid bills, Caruso sang personal arias for Yazedjian and of-

38

fered opera tickets as substitute currency. "My grandfather saw a great many nice operas," Damadian recalls, "but he was stuck for a lot of money when Caruso died."

Damadian's father, Vahan Krikor Damadian, an Armenian, was born in the small Turkish town of Kayseri in 1903. He and his family were caught squarely in the Turkish persecution of the Armenians. The Damadian family consisted of Vahan, then twelve, his sister, his mother, an aunt, and a cousin. Vahan Damadian's father had died several years before, and one day his uncle was forcibly removed from the household and presumably shot. They knew it was only a matter of time before the Turks would arrive at the house and hustle the family into a caravan of Armenians being herded on foot toward the Arabian desert. When that day came, they were allowed to hire a donkey and cart in order to take what they wanted with them, though it was clear to them that once they reached the desert, they would be killed. For forty days, they straggled along with some three hundred fellow Armenians. In the course of the treacherous march, Vahan contracted typhus and nearly died. Whille waiting to be shipped from Damascus to Der Zoar, a soldier came looking for the Damadian family with a special order. It turned out to be a permit issued by the Secretary of the Interior of Turkey. As it happened, Vahan had an uncle in Constantinople, and on the strength of some powerful friendships he had been able to secure the order saving the Damadians. "It was an incredible miracle," Vahan Damadian recalls. "On the verge of being shipped away, we were snatched from probable death."

The soldier hired a coach and escorted the family to Aleppo, Syria, where Vahan's mother found a Christian family who agreed to rent them a room. His mother and sister worked in a makeshift factory spinning thread that was then used to make socks and sweaters for the soldiers. In return, they were paid with huge pots of vegetables and tomatoes.

Vahan pitched in by working as a money changer out on the streets, his clients German soldiers stationed in Aleppo who needed to exchange gold for native currency.

When the war ended in 1918, the Damadians heard from two of Vahan's brothers who lived in the United States, where they plied the rug trade. Learning of the holocaust, they began searching for the family. Through the American Red Cross and other relief organizations, they managed to track them down in Aleppo and sent money to buy them passage to America. The Damadians departed in 1920 and went to Bridgeport, Connecticut, where they stayed with one of the brothers. Vahan worked in a lace factory and then at a silversmith shop making expensive silver. In 1927, the family moved to New York, where the second brother lived. Vahan took up photoengraving, working at the *New York World*, which later became the *World-Telegram*.

Soon after settling in New York, Vahan went hunting for a wife. In short order, he met Odette at a supper dance in New York thrown by the Armenian Junior League. They liked each other at once—they had an instinctive certainty that they were meant for each other—and were married in 1932.

The young couple was living in Manhattan when Raymond Damadian was born on March 16, 1936. His mother had lost her first child at childbirth; Raymond was her second. (A sister, Claudette, would be born a year and a half later.) Soon after his birth, the family relocated to Queens, eventually settling in Forest Hills. Forest Hills boasted something of an aristocratic community called Forest Hills Gardens that enveloped the West Side Tennis Club, long the fabled site of the United States Tennis Championships. Damadian grew up a good distance away from that community in a cozy little house on Austin Street.

"Now I think it's significant that I grew up there rather than in the aristocratic community," Damadian says. "Most of our neighbors were of Jewish descent, very much interested in traditional goals of scholarship and high achievement. This was not true of the aristocratic community, as I came to discover. These were sons and daughters of well-to-do people who would be taken care of regardless of what they achieved and inside of whose family the preeminent concern was social standing. I've never cared about social standing. It's never meant a thing to me."

Damadian attended P.S. 101, which was situated in Forest Hills Gardens. It was a remarkably good school with an ample sprinkling of brainy students and excellent teachers. It stimulated Damadian's already restless curiosity. As his mother remembers, "He was always interested in something creative. Drawing, reading, building. Everything was creative. He was always doing something. He could never sit still. If he did, he was reading."

Both of Damadian's parents played the violin and adored music, and so when Damadian was five his mother took him to Manhattan and enrolled him in violin lessons. From the very beginning, he demonstrated uncommon musical talent. When he was eight, his teacher urged him to go to Juilliard to continue his studies. He agreed to an audition. "It was kind of an amusing incident. I hadn't practiced in a while, which was one of my shortcomings. I hadn't practiced the violin in weeks, and when I took it out of the case the instructor couldn't tune it because the pegs were frozen. Everyone made much merriment of that. They finally tuned it, and I played and I was scared to death. I didn't even complete the entire audition, I was so terrified." Damadian left convinced that he would never hear from Juilliard again. About two weeks later, however, he received a call from an official at the school, who asked him brightly, "Raymond, how are we going to admit you to Juilliard if you don't complete the rest of your audition?" So he returned, finished the requirements, and was promptly admitted and assigned to Andrew McKinley.

Besides being a violin instructor, McKinley was an operatic tenor. (He is best known, however, for his part in the version of *Amahl and the Night Visitors* that turns up on television every year at Christmastime. McKinley plays Caspar, one of the three wise men, who brings a jewel box for the Nativity.) McKinley recalls Damadian: "He was a favorite of mine. Among the many people I taught in my lifetime, he stood out, I would say, mainly for personality reasons. He was always so honest and straightforward and kindly. . . . He always had a lot of self-confidence. But I never found in him confidence that was egotistical. A lot of these people, when they have great self-confidence, it's obnoxious. I never got that from him. I used to just love to see him walk in the room."

A belief in God and the rituals associated with that belief were a central part of Damadian's upbringing. Much of his social life took place at church. "He learned that you have to give and take," his mother says. "He learned life. He became religious, but not a fanatic."

Both of Damadian's parents played tennis with considerable panache, and, as with their proclivity toward music, they imbued their son with their interest. When he turned twelve, Damadian became a junior member of the West Side Tennis Club. He plunged into tennis; he took innumerable lessons with the resident professional, a fairly well-known pro named George Agutter, who had competed against the likes of Bill Tilden. Agutter subscribed to a style of play that was then novel but would eventually emerge as the favored method of modern players. Simply put, his technique was to come around at the ball and strike it with a forward roll of the wrist to give it some topspin. The prevailing style of the day was to swat at the ball with a flat stroke. The topspin approach allowed a strong player to pound the ball with tremendous force yet still keep it within the confines of the court, a difficult feat with a flat smash. "I got very good quickly," Damadian says of his tennis exploits. "I won the junior championship many times at the club. I played Junior Davis Cup."

Early on, Damadian displayed the zest and relentless determination that was to keep his fires stoked later in life. Winning was important to him. One of his closest childhood friends was a puckish fellow named Charles Brukl. He shared Damadian's passion for tennis. Brukl was a grade behind Damadian in school, but since he was also among the better players at the West Side Tennis Club, he and Damadian became close buddies and several times teamed to win the junior doubles championship. They also found themselves pitted against one another in singles. "We were both very fierce competitors on the tennis courts," Brukl says. "He used to get very mad if I beat him, and I used to get very mad at him if he beat me. I have salted away some pretty funny before-and-after photographs of our matches. Before this one match we were all smiles. After the match, which I won, I was still all smiles and he looked like he had just lost his entire family in a plane crash."

"Charlie was a gifted athlete," Damadian says. "His ground strokes were terrible. He'd hit a backhand over the fence; you'd hit to his forehand and you wouldn't know where the ball would go. But he'd hit these shots and come loping up to the net and you just couldn't get the ball past him. He'd leap in the air like a gazelle. So he'd hit this creampuff at me and I'd plaster it down the line and he'd bomb it back at me. But he had a volatile temperament. If you got him into a situation where he'd blow an easy shot, he'd go into a terrible rage and he was finished for the set. I remember one match when we were playing for the junior championship and I gave him a lob and he missed it and went into such a rage that he threw his racket up in the air and it didn't come back. Hedges served as a backstop, and they must have gone up sixteen feet. Charlie's racket was up in the hedges.

"The last match we played was a five-set match in hundred-and-five-degree heat. I was down two sets. It was a duel. I won the next two sets, and I thought I was going to win the match. Then, in the fifth set, I got cramps all over my body, and it was hopeless. I was falling all over the court. It was just unbelievably hot. It was a long, arduous deal. So I was losing games and I thought, What a bad thing and why doesn't it happen to him? Why doesn't he get a charley horse? And I looked across the net and he was holding the racket very loosely. He had a charley horse in his hand. But I had it much worse. So I lost. That was the one time he beat me back in those days."

Summers, when not smashing overheads, Damadian occupied his time with a succession of diverse jobs. One year he worked for one of his father's friends at his rug-cleaning factory. Boredom quickly did him in. All he seemed to do was lug heavy rugs around, and so every chance he could he stole off, deposited himself on a pile of carpets, and was lured into sleep. Another summer, he was employed as a soda jerk at a Howard Johnson's. He found the job exasperating. Before he even got in the door to start his stint, people were shrieking their orders at him. "Then he hit on the idea of selling cutlery," Charlie Brukl says. "It was pretty good cutlery—Cutco. You got these kits of knives and sold them door to door. He got me into this too. We did it for three or four weeks. He always seemed to be a better salesman than I was. After I exhausted all of my mothers' friends, one set each, my business came to a screeching halt. But he always seemed to be able to sell some of the half sets and find new prospects."

Both Damadian children got along well and were generally well behaved. Damadian's principal early offense—he has not outgrown it—was to come home late. If the curfew were midnight, he would be certain to straggle in at one. Infractions were the province of Damadian's mother. "Their father didn't discipline them; I disciplined them," his mother says. "My discipline was to put them in their room. They were not to come out until they said what they did. To Raymond, discipline didn't matter much, because he would just take out a book or do some work. He was never at a loss for something to do. I never knew whether sending him to his room did any good."

One somber event did leave an indelible impression on the young Damadian and many years later would release a stable of emotions. One of his grandmothers lived with the family on Austin Street. "She was a very sweet lady," Damadian says. "She adored us. She was French, and very French in style. She was a strict disciplinarian. But she was a sucker for the grandchildren. She was the one we always ran to for shelter when my mother was in a disciplinary mood. She took us to movies and spent a lot of time teaching me to read. I remember sitting on her lap and going over the reading book with her and her being impatient when I didn't get it right."

When Damadian was ten she contracted cancer in her left breast and died a slow and painful death. "The last few months were very bad," his mother says. "She was in pain all the time. But she pleaded not to be put in the hospital. It was very hard. When you have your children run downstairs and say, 'Mommy, do something for Grandma—she's suffering,' that has to leave an impression on you. That happened frequently." She died in 1946. "Afterward, Raymond asked me what she had," his mother says, "and I told him cancer. He wondered if she could be cured. I think that's when he got it into his head that he wanted to cure cancer."

"It was terrible," Damadian remembers. "She used to just lie there and moan—'Ohhhhhh, ohhhhhh, ohhhhhh.' She had her own room on the second floor, and my mother had a hospital bed for her, and during the last few months there was a full-time nurse. She had a terrible cancer of the breast. It was very swollen and red. It was gangrenous and there was a big cavity in it. It smelled terrible. She just lay there for months and moaned all the time. She would scream in pain in the middle of the night. She was getting pain medication, but still she moaned. During that time we didn't go out as a family. Someone had to stay with her. Everything focused on taking care of Grandma. For a long time, I didn't know she was going to die. It wasn't until I asked the nurse one day when Grandma was going to get well, and the nurse said she wasn't going to. Her suffering had a strong impact on me. I had an early exposure to the ravages of cancer. I saw very clearly what that horrid disease could do. For months after she died, I could still hear that moaning. Grandma was gone, but the moaning wouldn't seem to go away. I'd keep hearing it night after night after night."

School came relatively easy to Damadian. "I was a good student. I wasn't number one at P.S. 101, but I remember being disappointed at not being chosen valedictorian. I went to Forest Hills High School and had a ninety-three average. I was good in math and science. At the time, Forest Hills High School had the record for capturing the most Westinghouse Science Talent Search Awards, outstripping Bronx Science." Damadian recalls with fondness Wally Manheim, his trigonometry instructor, who fired Damadian's interest in math. "He used to come into the class and play us blindfolded in chess and beat us. And we had some smart kids. There was one kid who was twelve years old and used to sit up on telephone books to take his tests."

All this time, Damadian was still under the spell of the violin, and he gave periodic recitals and seriously pondered music as a career. Then he qualified for the Ford Foundation scholarships at the age of fifteen. The program allowed students to enter college before they had completed high school. Four universities participated in the awards—the University of Wisconsin, the University of Chicago, Columbia, and Yale. Grants for full tuition and room and board were bestowed on the winners. Some ten thousand students were nominated along with Damadian; they were winnowed down to two hundred. Damadian was picked to go to Wisconsin.

Naturally, he was delighted, yet at the same time he was torn, because accepting the scholarship meant turning his back on a musical career. One of the first things he did was to ask Andrew McKinley for advice. Should he go to Wisconsin and forget music? Or should he remain in high school and then proceed to Juilliard? Damadian's parents didn't have the money to send him away to college, so the Ford Foundation scholarship was more than just a tempting opportunity.

McKinley pointed out that it would be extremely difficult for Damadian to make it as a concert violinist. "It wasn't that hard a decision," Damadian says. "If I didn't accept the scholarship, it wouldn't be possible to go away to school at all, because we didn't have the financing. But I did think about it. The other thing was whether I had the talent to appear on the concert stage, because I wasn't interested in playing in a symphony. It's boring. One of the things about playing the violin is you get to hear your own music and you're creating something. In a symphony, you're one of a hundred people. You can't even hear your own music. When I talked it over with McKinley, he said, 'You can count the people on the concert stage on one hand and I don't think you're likely to be one of them.' There was a prodigy at Juilliard when I was there who was fifteen. He was playing all over the place. He was playing with major symphonies on all the concert stages. And I just wasn't in his league." And so he packed his bags for the Middle West.

At Wisconsin, Damadian majored in math and minored in chemistry. By the time he had finished his sophomore year he had decided that he wanted to go on to medical school. He roomed with three other male students; they used to refer to themselves as the "Four D's," because three of them had last names beginning with D and the fourth's first name was Don. Wisconsin boasted a stellar football team at the time, which included Alan Ameche, who would go on to professional stardom as the fullback for the Baltimore Colts. Damadian and Ameche became friends. Among other common traits, both of them sported prominent noses, and they would tease each other mercilessly about them.

Damadian went on to Albert Einstein Medical School, then a brand-new college that was part of Yeshiva University. The choice is simply explained: "It was the first and the best medical school I got into." At Einstein, unlike in his past academic life, Damadian's star shone at no more than half its potential luminosity. Many years later, Damadian can explain why: "Medical schools are highly disciplined environments that put a creative person at a disadvantage. The creative mind tends to automatically associate new facts being presented with past facts he had learned. In the mathematical analogy, I refer to this as the associative brain that tends to automatically associate and correlate facts loaded in memory as opposed to a commutative brain that just takes facts and flips them back and forth. For someone with a commutative brain, a fact learned is a fact stored. It's just like loading memory in a computer. A person with a creative mind, on the other hand, is not comfortable with new information until that new information first makes peace with the other information already stored in memory. The classic reaction of the creative mind when two associated facts don't jibe is 'I don't understand.' And he won't be able to learn either until the new information makes peace with that other information already locked in memory. I had a lot of trouble making peace between the information presented to me in medical school and the math and physics I had learned as an undergraduate."

He laughs for a moment. Then he continues. "I remember a most embarrassing incident. I remember a professor calling out from the lectern, without warning, during a class in microbiology, 'Damadian, what kind of medium do you grow the tuberculosis bacillus on?' It would never even have occurred to me to bother to store away such a ridiculous fact. The answer was Tween enriched Dubos 80 medium. It's really a bunch of nonsense words. And there must have been a hundred and fifty different growth media for bacteria. I did not know the answer. And I surely was the fool for it. The only reason that I know it now is because of that incident. I never used it again. That's the kind of nonsense thing we learned."

Money being tight, Damadian was obliged to find summer work to foot the bills for his medical education. His best ticket seemed to be his skill with a tennis racket, and so in 1956 he turned professional and landed a job as the teaching pro at the Dune Deck Hotel in Westhampton, Long Island. A mile or so down the beach, his old buddy Charlie Brukl was teaching at the Westhampton Bath and Tennis Club, a coincidence that would allow for many mirthful experiences. The two of them roomed together in a private house not far from the clubs. It was a sumptuous setting in which to spend one's summers. The hotel perched right on the ocean. The beach was magnificent. Had he had his druthers, Damadian would have chosen to devote his summers to research, but instead he got $2,500 a season to smooth out the backhands and errant serves of members of the club. He worked hard for it. He taught eight hours a day and also gave a string of exhibitions.

Brukl remembers those summers: "Both of us were very good teachers, and we had our own special clientele. That area was well populated with very wealthy and well-known people. Damadian played against and taught both Jacob Javits and his brother. They were pretty good tennis players. When they came down to the beach, they always wanted to play against two pros, so he used to call me and say, 'I've got the Javitses here,' and we used to play doubles against them. We always beat them. We bought the first car that either of us ever owned out there. It was a 1947 Studebaker for which we paid the grand sum of fifty dollars, twenty-five each. It threw out these huge clouds of blue smoke. He used to use the car to commute from Forest Hills to Albert Einstein, and the thing died on him one day at about two or three o'clock in the morning on the Triboro Bridge. They wanted to charge him more to tow the car away than it was worth. I remember that I was always more mechanically inclined than he was. I really was in later years surprised that he got into the area of medical research that he did, because he wasn't that gifted mechanically. But he was the kind of guy who could have been good at anything. He always seemed to know what was going on with whatever he was studying. If he had wanted to pursue a tennis career, he could have become one of the best tennis players in the United States."

There was, as it happened, no time to even think about competing in tennis tournaments, which is probably just as well. As Damadian recalls, "I still thought about playing tennis professionally, and I probably could have done it. One consideration was that tennis pros then made a meager existence. Most of the big competitions were for amateurs. Most people who looked forward to becoming tennis professionals looked forward to becoming tennis bums."

During breaks in their regimen, Damadian and Brukl used to traipse into Westhampton in search of good times. They often stopped for sodas at Speed's Pharmacy. The soda jerk on duty there was a quiet, fetching young woman named Donna Terry. Brukl started dating her, while Damadian went out with a co-worker of hers. Often they would double-date. "Ray would spend the entire evening playing the guitar and singing, and I thought he was a lot of fun," Donna says. "The next summer, he asked Charlie if he could ask me out, and Charlie said all right, and so I started going out with Raymond. He was always fun. He just seemed to be different from anyone else I had been with. He was a medical student and he was a tennis pro, and tennis was the one sport I never seemed to be able to master."

While school was in session, music continued to rouse Damadian's interest. He organized a group of fellow students with good vocal cords and formed an octet that he called the Lymph Notes. As well as singing lead tenor, Damadian arranged many of the songs they performed, which included such popular standards as "If I Loved You" and "The Wiffenpoof Song." During the year, the group would perform at dances or serenade nursing students of Columbia Presbyterian or Cornell Medical Center in their dormitories. The group was good enough to catch the attention of some people at CBS Records, who wanted them to cut a promotional record that could be distributed to medical organizations. CBS offered the then extremely handsome sum of $150,000. The Lymph Notes, however, needed the permission of the school brass to use the Albert Einstein name. Though the group intended to donate the full remuneration to the university for student scholarships, officials nixed the idea. Payola scandals were then rocking the record industry, and everyone was a bit skittish.

In 1960, a week after Damadian graduated from medical school, he and Donna Terry got married. They moved into a cramped, somewhat shabby apartment near Columbia. As Damadian describes it, "We had a three-room apartment at sixty-five dollars a month that we shared with the roaches. The number of roaches was incredible. I remember hearing a noise in the kitchen one night and I went in there and saw a cupboard door being swung open by a mass of roaches. I shrugged and went back to bed."

As his medical education proceeded, Damadian found himself increasingly disposed toward large-scale subjects. "I took an interest in mass immunology. I became intrigued by the idea of transplanting organs. I dreamed up various schemes of immunizing animals so you could transplant organs. It seemed terribly important to me. I had to be drawn to things that seemed important to me." It became clear to him that he would go into internal medicine. "I chose it because it was the most analytical of the disciplines where chemistry came into play. It was the most fun. It was solving puzzles. The internist is the puzzle solver of medicine. The surgeon does his thing. The obstetrician delivers babies. But it's the internist who tries to solve the peculiar diagnostic problem. He's the sleuth of medicine."

By the time he was ready to graduate, Damadian had changed his mind a few more times and finally chose research as his path to future glory. "I guess I decided I had the possibility of making an important contribution to medicine. I realized that a scientist who goes into the laboratory has the capability to help millions of people before his time is spent, whereas the practitioner of medicine can help only the few thousands he comes into direct contact with in the course of his career. I didn't know if anything would come of any research I might do, if anything at all would come of it, but I knew I wanted the chance to try to help those millions of people."

FIVE

In his office at Johns Hopkins University Hospital, both his legs outstretched, Donald Hollis put aside Damadian's 1971 *Science* article on NMR and rolled its fundaments over in his mind. Hollis had a happy-go-lucky voice and the air of a born charmer. He was a medical researcher, caught up by NMR explorations of biological systems, and he carefully pondered any discovery of note in the field. It was thus inevitable that Damadian's step into the unknown was going to fire up some engines in Baltimore, Maryland, where Hollis worked.

Hollis grew up in the state of Washington and majored in chemistry at the University of Puget Sound. He went on to do graduate work at Stanford University, where his mentor was Richard Ogg, Jr., an NMR expert of some note. After graduating from Stanford in 1959, with a taste for NMR, Hollis got a job at Varian Associates, a maker of electronic instruments in nearby Palo Alto. Varian had recently set up a division to make NMR machines, and Hollis's role at the company was to introduce scientists in industry to the technology. He published a number of papers on problems in NMR and helped spread awareness of what was still a relatively unknown concept. In 1964, Hollis was offered an appointment at Johns Hopkins Medical School, which was in the process of getting an NMR machine and establishing the first NMR laboratory in a medical school. Hopkins needed someone well tutored in the technology to run the device and interpret the resulting data. Hollis jumped at the opportunity. "I liked Varian, but I was interested in the biological and medical side of NMR," he says.

At first, Hollis's curiosity drifted to studying metal-containing enzymes. Among the medical students who worked with him was a particularly energized individual named James Economou. Hollis, who is more imperturbable in temperament, characterizes him like this: "He wanted to be a surgeon and specialize in cancer. His lifetime ambition was to cure cancer. He was a hotshot and a young kid and he thought he could do it." When Damadian's *Science* paper came out, Economou read it. It was an eye-opener and it added a strong fillip of energy to his normal rarefied state. As Hollis recounts it, "He came rushing in and said this guy said you can detect cancer, but who cares about rats, let's do it in humans. So I sat down and read Damadian's paper closely, and except for suggesting that you could detect cancer, it didn't make much sense." Among other things, Hollis, like the better part of the scientific community, reacted to Damadian's references to the radical structured-water belief with a mixture of amusement and derision. "It's a totally harebrained theory," he scoffed. "It's just madness."

Hollis and Economou determined that they would test Damadian's results and, if they proved correct, explore the subject further. At that time, Hollis was not yet in a position to duplicate the experiments on his own NMR machine. Thus at the tail end of the summer, a year after Damadian left, he and Economou arranged to visit New Kensington. They took with them four rats. They were escorted to a machine and spent a day or two testing tissue samples.

Hollis was not terribly comfortable hanging around NMR Specialties too long. He preferred doing his work in a reasonable amount of privacy, and at the company secretaries and technicians were constantly meandering through the place, looking over everyone's shoulder. (They were also occasionally gasping and shrieking because of the seemingly crude method being used to kill the rats. Since it was important not to allow foreign substances to invade the tissue, they could not give the rats chloroform or some other drug. Economou would grab a rat by the tail, swing it through the air, and smash its head crisply against a table edge, instantly killing it.)

Hollis's results compared favorably with Damadian's, which was enough stimulus for him to return to Johns Hopkins and delve further into the matter. He was not, at that point, especially excited about the ramifications. A decidedly cautious man by nature, he wanted to see a lot more extensive experimentation. Unlike Damadian, he wasn't willing to engage in visionary leaps to machines that would scan the human body.

At the time of Hollis's experiments, a mild-mannered, forty-two-year-old chemist happened to be in town who came to play a significant role in the development of NMR imaging in medicine. He would also come to be credited by a host of fellow chemists as the true founding father and driving force of the field. To Damadian, he would become a nemesis; to this day, he is barred from ever visiting Damadian's laboratories. No name incites more fury in Damadian than Paul Lauterbur. At the same time, Paul Lauterbur is not abundant in his admiration for Raymond Damadian, seeing him as a prickly outsider to the old-line NMR community. Over the years, the two have fired a good many astringent salvos at each other. The history of science brims with episodes of nasty bickering between rival scientists over credit for major discoveries. It was small wonder, then, that the retelling of the events leading to the development of NMR as a medical detection tool would stir up the sort of name-calling and bitterness that often results from king-size scientific egos.

Paul Lauterbur was born in 1929 in the tiny town of Sidney, Ohio, some forty miles from Dayton. He was the son of a mechanical engineer. Always infatuated by science as a child, he says he more or less flipped a coin to decide whether to pursue a career in physics or chemistry. Chemistry won. He got an undergraduate degree in chemistry from Case Institute of Technology. After he graduated in 1951, he was named a fellow at the Mellon Institute in Pittsburgh, where he undertook research into the properties of silicone for Dow Corning. In 1953, when manpower was being drafted for the Korean War, Lauterbur was called into the Army and assigned to the Army Chemical Center in Edgewood, Maryland.

As it happened, the Army had acquired an NMR machine. No one knew much about it, and Lauterbur had never seen one. When he was at Mellon, however, he began hearing scattered talk about some of the applications of NMR techniques to chemistry. Lauterbur thus started inquiring about NMR as something that could be helpful to his silicone work. One day, Lauterbur told a fellow soldier in the barracks about his interest in NMR, and the soldier passed the information on; before long Lauterbur found himself transferred to the NMR lab. The Army planned to use the machine to investigate the complex chemistry of nerve gas and other chemicals deployed in warfare. "It was not the sort of thing I would have chosen to work on," Lauterbur says, "but I was drafted and that was the laboratory to which I was assigned, and so that's the way things went." Lauterbur and colleagues in the lab conducted a number of NMR surveys of such materials as phosphorus compounds and exotic boron compounds. "So we weren't really doing Army work in the sense that we weren't putting hand grenades containing toxic gases into our machine."

After he was discharged from the Army, Lauterbur felt he wanted to continue doing NMR work, since he saw it as a valuable technique for a chemist to use in unlocking the secret of compounds. "The problem in chemistry is you take one flask of a substance and mix it with a second flask of a substance and create a third substance. How do you know what you've got? What is the structure of what you've done? These are questions you ask every day in the chemistry laboratory." The Dow Corning group that had sponsored Lauterbur's work at Mellon agreed to acquire a machine so that Lauterbur could, among other things, study organic silicon compounds. He soon found out that he could do studies of carbon NMR spectra, which were of far greater interest to him. "Carbon opens up the whole field of organic chemistry and biology, too, so we opened up the whole field of carbon spectroscopy."

Eventually, Lauterbur got around to finishing his doctorate requirements at the University of Pittsburgh, and in February 1963 he left to set up a program to do NMR studies in chemistry at the State University of New York at Stony Brook. For the balance of the 1960s, Lauterbur studied various subtle questions of how molecules behaved, including explorations of carbon-13 and aluminum borohydride. He then became captivated by biological areas and took a year's sabbatical to learn a bit more about the subject at Stanford University. As he expresses it, "That's what academic sabbaticals are for, to get away from the mess on your desk to look at some new perspectives."

Since he had established himself as a powerful voice in NMR research, it was not surprising that Lauterbur was invited to become a member of the board of directors of Nuclear Magnetic Resonance Specialties. By the early 1970s, however, the company found itself hopelessly mired in financial difficulties. Paul Yajko himself was squeezed out of the president's office; Yajko, in fact, would ultimately flee the sciences and go on to become, of all things, a garlic farmer and would start a business to reclaim precious metals in Pennsylvania. Searching for a way to save the company from ruin, the directors asked Lauterber to take over the helm during the summer of 1971. As it turned out, the company had sunk into even sorrier shape than Lauterbur imagined. He questioned the proprieties of some of the practices that came to light. He likes to tell how one of the bankers he used to deal with used to carry a business card that read: "The Jewish Godfather. I'm a Reasonable Man." Having been named president and chairman of the company, Lauterbur found himself facing this mess in New Kensington in early September of 1971, the same time that Hollis happened to ride into town.

Lauterbur remembers the events well. He had seen some of the readings being done on the rats by Economou, and he was intrigued by the experiments. A candle was lit. One evening, he and the personable Don Vickers, as was often their night-time habit, went out to grab some dinner at a nearby Eat 'n' Run restaurant, a hamburger joint that specialized in a double-decker burger called a Big Boy. For some time, the two sat conversing idly, and Luaterbur, during the stillnesses, dug into his imagination, until he struck something that won his entire attention. This is how Lauterbur tells of that evening:

"I had watched some of those experiments being done. And they were seeing some differences between the cancerous tissue and the normal tissue. A phenomenon seemed to be at work there. But I couldn't imagine that it was very likely that it would be important to do such investigations of tissue. A method that required cutting out the samples didn't seem all that interesting. From what little I knew, I thought you could probably characterize biopsy sample better by microscopic investigation. But it did seem useful if you could take measurements from the intact human body and create images. So I got to asking myself whether there was any conceivable way of solving this problem. So I went out that evening to the local Eat 'n' Run restaurant—sort of the local equivalent of McDonald's—and I sat down to munch on a Big Boy. Sitting in a lonely hamburger joint and thinking hard.

"And I got to thinking that magnetic field gradients provide a general solution to this problem. The reason you couldn't tell the different tissues in a normal NMR machine is that you make a magnetic field that's the same everywhere. If you have a magnetic field that is different on one side of the sample from another side, then the frequencies of the spectra are different, too. In a uniform field, if you have a little bit of tissue here and a little bit of tissue there, then the signal is the same, and if you plot that out the signals would be right on top of each other and you couldn't distinguish one from the other. Now, if you have a smoothly varying magnetic field, then you would have different frequencies and so you could study the signals and distinguish the differences.

"Now, this is one-dimensional. We're dealing with a three-dimensional object. So the question was, Could you extend this idea to resolve completely the three-dimensional object? I thought that if you could figure out how to do the mathematical manipulations, you should be able to go all the way."

Lauterbur's idea, as he eventually puzzled it out over a period of months, was, in essence, to superimpose on the uniform magnetic field a smaller, adjustable field that varied across the patient. This adjustable field, or linear field gradient, would give each part of the patient a different magnetic history, and the corresponding slight differences in the NMR resonance frequencies could be used by a computer to distinguish areas of the body in order to construct an image.

Lauterbur talked the idea out with Vickers. As Vickers has said, "This was a realization that he had in the space of about ten or fifteen minutes that fell on him like a ton of bricks." He polished off his Big Boy and went off to bed. The next day he scribbled down his idea about gradients in a tan spiral notebook, suggesting in his notes that it could allow NMR images to be done of the body and therefore serve as an application of Damadian's research. He asked Vickers to sign his notebook as a witness to his idea, a common safeguard in scientific work when a researcher believes he may have stumbled upon a patentable discovery. Lauterbur would later recount that he thought at the time that he had hit upon a "crackerjack of an idea."

"He was excited about it," Vickers said. "He was real excited about it. My attitude was, Hey, yeah, that's worth a shot. That's certainly something that ought to get chased."

Lauterbur told me the story of his breakthrough at his orderly, fluorescent-lighted office in the graduate chemistry building at Stony Brook. Even the blackboard that hung on one wall had been neatly erased. Lauterbur is a slightly pudgy man, with thinning gray hair and a beard. He has a crinkly-eyed smile. His secretary was tardy, so he found himself, in addition to answering his own calls, scribbling down messages for her. Lauterbur was gazing out his fifth-floor window at the campus below, students languorously making their way to class, when I said to him that it was really a remarkable combination of chance events—Damadian coming to NMR Specialties to attempt his experiments, Hollis being stimulated by the resulting paper and showing up there because he didn't have his own equipment ready, he being asked to run the company at the same time that Hollis was in town—that converged to steer him to his discovery.

"Yes," Lauterbur replied, "but life is full of things like that. If you turn left instead of right at the corner, you might not meet your wife."

At the time that he ate his momentous Big Boy, Lauterbur said that he had no inkling that Damadian had evolved any ideas about scanning the human body or fashioning a machine that could search through the body for disease; about all he had heard, he said, was that Damadian was looking into launching a company that would manufacture devices earmarked for use in hospitals that would test biopsy samples.

Damadian, of course, was talking about much more than that. (Vickers himself says, "I think it was common knowledge at this time, at least throughout New Kensington, that Ray Damadian wanted to stuff people into NMR machines.") He had clearly spelled out his intentions in several grant proposals, mentioned them in a letter to President Nixon, and informed a journalist of his plans. Unlike Lauterbur, however, Damadian was not at this time thinking about making pictures with an NMR machine. Imaging, specifically, had not occurred to him, and he would not begin to contemplate its importance until Lauterbur proposed his technique. Damadian was most intensely interested in gathering chemical data that would reveal diseased states; he viewed imaging, when he began to think about it, as just one of the subsidiary usages of the chemical maps obtained by NMR scanners.

Lauterbur's discovery changed his life. He resigned from NMR Specialties, which not long after ignominiously collapsed, and returned to Stony Brook. There, he says, he eventually perfected his imaging technique, working out the mathematics and physics of sculpting the magnetic field so that a properly programmed computer could unscramble the mysterious signals and reconstruct an image. Because his method of producing an image required that the object interact with two magnetic fields, a static one that has a superimposed linear magnetic gradient and one alternating at radio frequencies, he eventually gave his technique the weird-sounding name "zeugmatography," derived from the Greek word *zeugma*, meaning "joining." It would prove to be superior in producing images to the FONAR method, since it collected data a plane at a time rather than a point at a time, and the faster the image is gotten the clearer it is; even Damadian would, for a time in later years, make use of it. Damadian's method, on the other hand, was superior for gathering chemical information to help diagnose suspicious tissue seen on an image.

Details of Lauterbur's technique for imaging were eventually published in the March 16, 1973, issue of *Nature* magazine, along with the first NMR image ever made. Achieved on a conventional NMR device that had been somewhat modified for the purpose, the image was of two tiny tubes of water immersed in a larger tube. The paper, as it was initially submitted, was rejected by *Nature*, in large part because Lauterbur had outlined no application of the imaging technique. As he puts it, "They wanted to see something more than this funny idea." So, in a revision, he tacked on the suggestion that the technique could be used to distinguish between malignant and normal tissue, writing: "A possible application of considerable interest at this time would be to the in vivo study of malignant tumors, which have been shown to give proton nuclear magnetic resonance signals with much longer water spin-lattice relaxation times than those in the corresponding normal tissues."

However, Lauterbur did not see fit to reference Damadian's paper, but rather some subsequent experiments performed by several other researchers that corroborated what Damadian had suggested; only in later years would Lauterbur acknowledge that Damadian's work first triggered his interest. When asked why he chose not to bestow credit at the time, his explanation was that he decided to cite experiments that he was more familiar with. Damadian, however, read sinister motives into the omission, and he became convinced that Lauterbur was out to steal his discovery, a charge that Lauterbur has vigorously denied. A footnote to a scientific article may not seem like much, but scientists depend on references to their work to nourish their reputations and help them win grant money.

Damadian, as it happened, didn't see the *Nature* article

when it came out. Afterward, he periodically heard about some NMR technique called zeugmatography that was being promoted by Paul Lauterbur. He didn't know what in the world it was and, because of some misguided information, was not inclined to find out. Someone who told him about it led him to believe it had to do with two-dimensional analysis of chemical spectra, something not of much interest to Damadian. Then Lauterbur gave a speech sometime late in 1973 at Brooklyn College and a professor of chemistry there who was chummy with Damadian called him to report on it. He said that he was surprised to learn that zeugmatography dealt with scanning the human body and that, judging from Lauterbur's remarks, he was leading people to believe he had invented the whole idea of a body scanner.

Damadian quickly got hold of Lauterbur's *Nature* paper. After reading it and finding no mention of his own work, he blew up. He phoned Cope, among others, and delivered an earful of venom. "Here I was talking about medical scanning and getting ridiculed and here was this guy standing up and saying that he had invented it. I was absolutely shocked. I couldn't believe it." The memory of the incident firmly screwed itself into a corner of his mind. It would torment him for years, heighten his nervousness, convince him that he was a target of organized persecution. A bad turn of events and some voice deep inside him would whisper that somehow Paul Lauterbur was behind it.

In a coffee room in the physics department at the University of Nottingham, a wavy-haired professor named Peter Mansfield sat down one morning in June 1972 to drink a cup of eye-opening coffee with Allan Garroway, a postdoctoral associate of his, and Peter Grannell, a research student in his lab. They had a problem to thrash out. The team had been doing NMR studies of various substances, and they were having quite a bit of success but had exhausted the materials that were immediately available in the lab. As Mansfield puts it, "We didn't have any more materials to pop into the machine. So we were wondering what to do with it. It was going well, and it was sort of a pity not to do something else with it."

"To quote one of your film stars," Mansfield subsequently explained, "we were all dressed up and nowhere to go."

Mansfield was born in London, the son of an inspector for the London Gas Company. He was attracted to cosmology and space travel and thought he was going to become a rocket engineer. While he was studying physics at London University in 1958, he needed to build something to satisfy his degree requirements, and he chose as his project a metal detector of the sort an archaeologist might take on an excavation, based on the principle of nuclear magnetic resonance. His professor was impressed enough with the detector to invite Mansfield to do graduate work in NMR. He forgot about space travel and took up a subject that would command his attention for the rest of his career.

As Mansfield sipped his coffee in Nottingham (according to his retelling of the events), various concepts jiggled around in his head, and then something fused together. "I was saying, 'What can we do with it? What is it good for?' It occurred to me in a flash around the coffee table that we could study the distribution of atoms linearly using gradients—basically do imaging." Mansfield says he was entirely unaware at this point that Paul Lauterbur had already had essentially the same idea. Mansfield, though, was not thinking specifically of medical applications; in the first paper he published on this in 1974, in fact, he didn't even make any mention of imaging. Rather, he wrote of a general method to use an NMR machine to detect the faces of crystals in samples that possessed them.

Garroway listened to Mansfield's brainstorm patiently, then was effusive with his reaction. "He almost fell off his chair with laughter," Mansfield said. "He thought it was preposterous." Grannell, in Mansfield's recollection, "sort of thought, My God, more things to do! He was my student, so he wasn't allowed to be skeptical. He did what I told him."

Right in the coffee room, Mansfield dashed to the blackboard and demonstrated the methodology to his companions. He later worked on the mathematics and convinced himself that it was doable. Once he realized he could achieve spatial imaging, he looked around for applications, and Damadian's tumor experiments were drawn to his attention. "So it certainly had an influence," he said. "I think Damadian's work had some influence on everyone." Learning that Lauterbur was plowing ahead with his imaging idea spurred him as well to concentrate all his efforts on medical imaging instead of crystallography.

Believing his idea had illimitable potential, Lauterbur spoke to a lawyer who worked with NMR Specialties about patenting it. While patent proceedings were set in motion, the attorney instructed Lauterbur to refrain from doing any experimentation on Stony Brook equipment, because it might compromise his claim, and so he postponed further tests of the idea. During this interlude, he approached several entrepreneurs about forming a company that someday might make human scanners, but the reaction was decidedly cool, because he had nothing more to offer at this stage than an interesting idea. "They wanted to know about the size of the market and return on investment and when production could start. You had to be able to see farther in the future than these chaps wanted to." Before the patent application had advanced very far, Lauterbur and his lawyer developed a serious breach over matters relating to NMR Specialties. "By now I was very anxious to go ahead and do some experiments," Lauterbur said. "I was chafing to get out from under the restrictions of the commercial patent application. So I said to hell with it and decided to do experiments." At the same time, Lauterbur presented his imaging idea to the Research Corporation, a national concern that acts as an agent for various universities in securing patents and was the representative for Stony Brook. It declined to pursue it. Its conclusion was that it was neither arresting enough nor profitable enough to be worth the time and expense of obtaining a patent. Lauterbur said that he subsequently asked the university for a release that would allow him to pursue once again a patent on his own but that "it never got around to doing it."

When Lauterbur talked about his imaging idea around Stony Brook, there was hardly a climate of support. The reactions of many of his colleagues were similar to the responses that were greeting Damadian. They thought he was crazed. Nevertheless, he attracted funding from the National Cancer Institute that allowed him to buy an NMR spectrometer, and he began assembling a team. The first key person he hired was Ching-Ming Lai, a graduate of Stony Brook's physics department, who would do a sizable amount of the imaging work in the lab. As Lai would later say, "Lauterbur had ideas, but as a chemist he didn't know about working the instruments or even the mathematics."

Lauterbur, meanwhile, energetically took his idea to scientific meetings here and abroad. He became a one-man traveling evangelical show, teaching the new religion of NMR imaging. Converting disciples at this early juncture, though, proved difficult. Titillating as his idea might seem on paper, the general consensus of the scientific community was that it was amusing to think that an NMR machine could possibly be designed that could make pictures of the inside of the human body. It was one of those dark scientific tunnels that would never come out of the ground. Lauterbur, pushing his product, managed to block out the nay-sayers and forge ahead, patiently waiting for the rest of the world to accept his truth.

SIX

Damadian went to his laboratory these days brimming with confidence. He walked with a jaunty air. Ideas swam in his head. He would talk at length to his two principal research associates, Michael Goldsmith and Larry Minkoff—in the lab, at lunch, at dinner—about the promise of NMR. He was a study in impatience, for already he was imagining lives being saved by what, in reality, was still an unproven concept. But he was a man with a mission. Confidence, he believed, was the essential ingredient of success, and he had it in abundance.

What concerned him, though, was a lack of money. In the past, his work had been funded by sundry grants from one scientific agency or another, but the money had now almost totally evaporated. The shortage of funds had been producing something of a treadmill mood in him. No matter how much he skimped, no matter how much he did himself, his material situation seemed not to improve at all.

In early 1971, he undertook a stubborn, largely fruitless hunt to attract funding from conventional scientific sources. He submitted an application to the Health Research Council of the City of New York, only to be told that any discussion of scanning the body by NMR was "meaningless." He applied to the National Institutes of Health for funds to study cancer detection through the use of NMR. He asked for a three-year budget: $18,784 the first year, $20,520 the second, and $13,256 the third. In June 1971, the application was rejected.

Disheartened but not disenchanted, he persisted in courting the government for money. Days after being notified of the NIH rejection, he dashed off an angry letter to President Nixon. The first paragraph ran: "I am writing to you because I have nowhere else to turn. Perhaps you are the only one with the wisdom and the imagination to put this matter straight." He wrote, "I stand here shaking my head in disbelief" that the NIH had turned down the proposal, and he added, "It seems necessary to say that we feel our findings represent one of the most powerful and exciting breakthroughs in cancer in the last 50 years." He went on to mention that his research "means that the way is open for the construction of a detector . . . which would contain a small probe that could be passed back and forth across the human body hunting down internal cancer deposits when they are still small enough to be obliterated by conventional therapy and specifying their anatomic location." He continued, "The rejection of my grant by the National Institutes of Health is a colossal stupidity. Failing to recognize the immense power of this breakthrough in cancer technology reflects only the enduring ignorance and the complete absence of vision of the men who decide." He ended, "I beg of you to intercede, Mr. Nixon, and see to it that this project is funded immediately. It is too important to permit delay."

In July, on the urging of one of the NIH administrators, Damadian submitted a fresh application to the agency, and, perhaps helped by the Nixon letter, he was funded in January for three years at an annual rate of $20,000. He used the money to buy his first NMR machine. He bought the spectrometer from NMR Specialties and the magnet from Westinghouse.

There are three types of magnets: permanent magnets of the sort you use to fasten grocery lists to the refrigerator door; resistive magnets, made out of many turns of copper wire and driven by an electrical power supply; and superconducting magnets. Damadian bought a superconducting magnet with a two-and-a-half-inch bore. A superconducting magnet is composed of tightly wound niobium-titanium wire that has to be cooled in a bath of liquid helium to almost absolute zero (minus 273.15 degrees centigrade), since it works on the principle that electrical resistance is totally eliminated in certain materials like niobium-titanium when they are cooled to temperatures approaching absolute zero. A high-amp input builds up the magnetic field in the coil, and then the coil is short-circuited with a built-in superconducting switch. Since the current now in the coil doesn't encounter wire resistance, it continues to flow independent of the power source. The field is extremely stable.

Keeping the magnet cooled, however, is tricky. Since helium at room temperature wants to be a gas, it must be contained in a sealed vessel known as a dewar. Even in a sealed container it steadily boils away at a rate of roughly one to two liters an hour. Helium costs something like $5 a liter. Buying helium, moreover, is not as simple as purchasing gasoline or heating oil. For the most part, the helium comes from the Arkansas gas and oil fields. It arrives in huge storage tanks, and it doesn't always arrive on schedule. Running out of liquid helium means ruining the magnet. It warms up, and the magnet becomes resistive. The energy in the magnet is converted to heat, and the leads and switches can melt. How fast can they melt? In perhaps twenty seconds. All the energy from the superconducting magnet is released as heat, and a puff of steam is discharged. Thus, it is necessary to order extra helium in advance, but not too far in advance, lest it will boil away before it ever gets used.

The magnet had to sit some three feet off the floor. Fresh liquid helium had to be poured in from above. The ceiling of the lab was simply too low to allow that, so Damadian managed to acquire the lab immediately below his. It was then necessary to turn the two spaces into the first duplex lab in

Downstate history. Shouldn't be too tough, Damadian reckoned. We can do it ourselves. Goldsmith and Minkoff gamely agreed.

A sledgehammer and chisel were obtained. *Crunch.* After repeated blows, no more than a two-inch hole was opened up. The floor was of poured granite a foot thick. They knew when they were licked. Two men with electric jackhammers were hired to finish the job.

Damadian and his students then had to build a platform for the magnet and an elevator to lower it so that it could be replenished with liquid helium. Then they built a staircase between the floors. Everything was ad-libbed. No one, for instance, was intimately acquainted with the building of staircases. One of the graduate students took a book out of the library on staircase design, and Damadian would stomp around the lab, poking through it, scratching his head, amazed at how complex a simple staircase could be. Every piece had a name—the tread, the overhang, the stringer. Since they would be dealing with a powerful magnet, they needed to use aluminum nails, which are apt to bend when driven into heavy lumber.

The various construction projects took on the appearance of a Marx Brothers movie. Goldsmith had the foresight to make them the subject of a half-hour home movie that he still shows periodically for his own amusement. Minkoff says of the time, "Mike said we were going to become slaves to our machine."

Damadian used his newly acquired magnet to study the differences in relaxation times of biopsy samples of cancerous and normal human tissues, the bulk of which he obtained from the prestigious Sloan-Kettering Memorial Cancer Center. In a paper that was eventually published in the April 1974 issue of *Proceedings of the National Academy of Sciences*, he reported on studies of twenty-eight different kinds of tumorous tissues. He found that breast tumors had a relaxation time of 1.080 seconds, three times longer than the mean time for normal breast tissue, 0.367 second. Cancerous lung tissue had a relaxation time of 1.110 seconds, compared with a mean for normal tissue of 0.788 second. The data he accumulated, which emerged in slow, painstaking fashion, helped him develop a framework from which he could one day build a human scanner.

By November 1973, the NIH funds had been exhausted by the high cost of liquid helium. With his new evidence of NMR's potential, Damadian resumed his efforts to acquire more backing. He made a series of submissions to the NIH, in particular to the National Cancer Institute, an arm of the agency, but all were unavailing. Five times he would apply to the American Cancer Institute; five times he would be rejected, told that the project was interesting but unfortunately too low in priority.

"Yeah, I sent grant applications to the American Cancer Society. You'd think they might be interested in cancer. And they rejected me. My sister's father-in-law was the owner of a Chinese restaurant in New York across from the Americana Hotel. I told him about my problems and he said he knew someone influential at the American Cancer Society who used to come into his restaurant. So I met the man and he arranged a meeting with Elmer Holmes Bobst, one of the founders of the American Cancer Society and the former head of Warner-Lambert. He had come up with the seven danger signs of cancer. He was ninety-three and he barely heard me. But he said he would try to help. So under Bobst's urging the American Cancer Society sent two people out to reevaluate the lab, one from NIH and one from Brookhaven. They said they were impressed with the work and would write a positive recommendation for funding. I got no answer and I finally called up and was told that the scientist at the American Cancer Society who hadn't liked the idea in the first place was very unhappy at the positive review I got and so he was going to have another review done. So he picks a guy who's close with Lauterbur and he came out and said this was ridiculous. He went back and wrote a negative report and I didn't get the money."

In his comfortless course through the world of grants, Damadian became increasingly convinced that because he was a maverick approaching the research differently than the members of the well-entrenched NMR community, people like Lauterbur and Hollis were subverting his efforts. The academic world, as he was quickly discovering, is a morass of monstrous egos and conflicts of interest. Every scientist seems to have his own filter of fact and fantasy. Progress was important, but only if you had a hand in it. Damadian became caught up in what he soon began to deride as the "appallingly disgusting" peer review system, in which scientists reviewed each other's grants. As Damadian says, "In the scientific community, reviewers commonly make nitpicking criticisms of research that they're jealous of and wish that they were doing. That's one of the greatest transgressions of science. It goes on every minute of every day. Finding objective reviewers who are free of all these biases is very difficult." As the rejections mounted, so did Damadian's contempt for his rivals. "They were hoping that I would just go away," he says. "I made the first discovery and then they figured, 'Okay, we'll take it from here.'"

Lauterbur, from Damadian's perspective, viewed Damadian as an outsider. He didn't have years of expertise in NMR, as Lauterbur did. He wasn't a chemist, as Lauterbur was. "I was looked on as a nebbish—a no-count." Damadian began to feel imprisoned, with Lauterbur as his warden.

Around this time, Lauterbur was scrambling to produce images using his NMR focusing technique. He did some so-called phantoms—glass tubes filled with water. He wanted to produce an image of a living creature, but the trouble was that the NMR machines were too small for many animals to fit into them. The inside diameter of the magnet he had was about four millimeters. What's more, the animal had to lie there quietly while an image was being constructed. As with a conventional photograph, movement blurred any image. An insect, for example, would fit into the machine easily, but its inclination would be to crawl away.

Lauterbur put his nine-year-old daughter to work. She foraged around the beach of Setawket Harbor, near where Lauterbur and his family were living, until one day she found a tiny clam, smaller than Lauterbur thought existed. Try this, Dad. It fit into the machine, and the resulting image was believed to be the first NMR image of a living creature. (The famous clam, alas, was subsequently lost someplace in the lab.) From the clam, Lauterbur went on to do images of nuts, tree branches, and, when he acquired bigger machines, a mouse and green peppers (the latter are interesting to image because they are hollow and thus have clear internal structures).

If Lauterbur was in fact hindering Damadian's efforts to raise money (Lauterbur professes to have had minimal impact), Donald Hollis was of no help, either. Once he returned to Johns Hopkins after duplicating Damadian's experiments in New Kensington, he began further NMR investigations of his own of malignant and benign tumors. He started to publish papers and issue comments at scientific gatherings that expressed considerable skepticism of the probable value of NMR in medicine. He became a tireless critic of Damadian, of whom he would later say, "I don't know that he's what you'd call a scientist. He's a businessman or a public relations expert." In the early 1970s, Hollis studied a half-dozen to ten different malignant tumors in various parts of a rat—the liver, kidney, brain, testicle, "everything you could think of in a rat"—and "we found that you couldn't even distinguish between some of the malignancies." He started examining human biopsy samples with his NMR machine and drew similar unpromising conclusions.

Damadian was beginning to realize that one of his problems was his visionary nature. He habitually made the mistake of presuming that others were as far-sighted as he was. "It's a question of having vision or not," he said one day while having lunch in a Long Island diner. "I can see these things. And when I see them, they're absolutely clear and sound. Most people, like Hollis, can't see beyond their noses. If I went out tomorrow to the beach and saw Russian submarines and saw Russian soldiers getting out on the beach and if I came back and said, 'I saw Russian soldiers landing on the beach,' ninety percent of the people would say I'm nuts. Ten percent of the people, those with sufficient imagination, would get up and run like mad out of here. It's the difference between people who have vision and those who don't. Trying to persuade people without vision is like trying to persuade a blind person to see. Cope used to tell me all the time that my visions were too large. 'Make them smaller.' I'd write up my grant proposals and show them to him and he'd say, 'Forget it, make it smaller.' Then I would rewrite it and come back and say, 'Okay, Freeman, this small enough?' He would look at it and reply, 'Are you crazy? Your eyes are still way too big.' I'm telling you that I can't think small enough. My brain just doesn't work that way. I see these things and they're vivid. They're real."

A scientist close to the efforts being made by Damadian to raise money once said: "Scientific administrators are basically spineless. They don't want to stick their necks out. They want to say what was popular. That's how they get their goodie-goodie points. So mediocrity reigns supreme. It took some guts [for Damadian] to do this."

Meanwhile, interest in NMR applications to medicine was

fired up in several laboratories throughout the world. Japanese scientists were interested. So were the Swiss, the English, the Russians. In 1973, a research team at the National Bureau of Standards managed to detect a cancerous tumor in the tail of a mouse. What's more, other NMR investigators were pocketing funds by riding Damadian's coattails. Donald Hollis has observed: "I think Damadian served as a foil. Unfortunately, the way science operates today, especially in the big university, the professors are supporting themselves. The scientist needs to get money. To get money, you need grantsmanship. Yet, on the other hand, you don't want to say anything outrageous that can come back to haunt you. So you report in your grant that NMR can be used to detect cancer and you reference Damadian. If this turns out wrong, well, you didn't say it, Damadian did. Others took advantage of the fact that he was willing to say these wild, outrageous things. In other words, it was popular to say that NMR could be used to diagnose cancer." Why, then, didn't Damadian get money? "Because he would write all this wild stuff in his grant applications," Hollis said, "whereas others would use his statements selectively. His would be laughed at. They were absurd."

Convinced that conventional channels would remain unavailing and that rival scientists were trying to piggyback on his talents, Damadian decided to take up the tin cup. In 1973, he set up a foundation that he called the Citizens' Campaign for New Approaches to Cancer. As Damadian remembers its inception, "We planned to raise huge amounts of money for all people doing cancer research." Damadian told his father about his foundation, and his father replied that he knew exactly how to drum up money. All they had to do was send out solicitations to wealthy members of the Armenian community. There were plenty of rich Armenians who would jump at the chance to help.

Damadian's father got a copy of the mailing list for the Armenian General Benevolent Union Presentation Ball, a gala debutante ball at which well-heeled Armenians introduced their daughters. A mailing was done to the six hundred people on the list. The mailing cost Damadian a dollar a name. A man who worked with Damadian's father and recognized the name sent fifty dollars. Three others chipped in five dollars apiece. Six hundred solicitations scared up a grand total of sixty-five dollars.

Before giving up, Damadian tried personal appeals to some noted Armenians he figured would not readily miss a few thousand dollars. He wrote to Kirk Kerkorian, the MGM kingpin. No response. Damadian picked up the phone and got one of Kerkorian's henchmen. The man just laughed. He tried a man in Detroit reputed to be worth three hundred million dollars. He was the inventor of the Delta faucet and ran the company that made the faucets. Not a tumble. He tried the family of a British-Armenian oil magnate said to have a billion dollars on hand. Not a cent. "The Armenians were not exactly my providers. They didn't give me the time of day."

At this point, Damadian's brother-in-law, David Terry, took up the cause. Terry had an enormous capacity for hard work. After he got out of high school, he enrolled in Mohawk Valley Community College but dropped out after half a year. The academic world seemed to him to be designed to make everything uninteresting. "It was boring to me. I was unmotivated and couldn't be bothered. I was looking out the window all the time." His family lived in East Quogue, Long Island, and so Terry moved to nearby Westhampton and found a job as a yardman in a lumberyard. He stuck with that for two and a half years, until he got sick of being so cold when he unloaded sheets of lumber off freight cars during the brittle Long Island winters. Terry was smoking at that time and he found that when he was out in the cold his legs would freeze and wouldn't thaw out for some hours. He quit and enrolled in a night course to learn the insurance business—his parents owned a small real estate and insurance agency in Quoque called the Carman-Terry Agency. Terry also completed a Dale Carnegie speaking course. He got a life insurance license and later a real estate broker's license and joined his parents' agency in 1967, when he was twenty.

For some people, it is their lot to work two jobs to make sufficient money to support themselves and their family. For a few rare people, it is their lot to work two jobs because no one career is enough to keep their life interesting. Terry is one of those latter types. Selling real estate and insurance by day, he played the drums in a band by night. The band was nothing if not versatile. It was equally at home performing at weddings and playing hard rock at Hampton wingdings. It called itself, during its wild nights, Lumpy Farina.

After two years, Terry laid aside the drumsticks and, for his second career, joined the Quogue police force. "I didn't do that for the money, either. I did that for the excitement. I always wanted to be a policeman. People trusted me. I was never a nasty cop. I only kicked in one door, and that was a hotel door during a fire. I didn't arrest a lot of people. I always tried to work things out. I learned some lessons that helped me later on. I found out that if you do your job right and arrest someone or give him a ticket because he deserved it, then when you take the handcuffs off or give him the ticket, he'll shake your hand. That would actually happen. Also, blood doesn't bother me today, and people in agony don't bother me. I saw it all." After a couple of years patrolling the streets, Terry quit the police force and shortly afterward took up his next part-time project. He assumed charge of the Citizens' Campaign for New Approaches to Cancer, which in its early months had raised not a penny.

Like Damadian, Terry possessed infectious enthusiasm. To his way of thinking, nothing seemed impossible. His eyes were big beyond the realm of reality. In an interview with *Newsday*, the Long Island daily, he said that the long-term goal of the Citizens' Campaign was to raise two million dollars for cancer research. The coffers would grow so immense that the money would be spread among numerous projects. Even though there was not yet enough money to purchase a chemistry set, Terry began to single out other scientists that he deemed worthy of support. He mentioned, for example, Dr. Anne Catherine Schmeer, the so-called Clam Nun of Bay Shore, Long Island. In 1962, she had discovered that certain types of clams from the waters of Long Island rarely, and perhaps never, developed malignant tumors. Subsequently, she claimed to have isolated the cancer-inhibiting agent, which she named "mercenene." She maintained that injections of the extract produced 80 to 100 percent regression of malignancy.

Damadian worked up a brochure that Terry used as his calling card. The cover showed an astronaut walking on the moon and declared: "Why can't the technology that put this man on the moon . . ." Opening to the next page, one was confronted with a fellow who appeared to be about thirty, his back turned, holding the hands of two young children. He was standing in a yard under a tree. The completion of the sentence ran above it: ". . . cure this man's cancer?" The man pictured in the photo was David Terry, who didn't really have cancer. The two children were his own son and daughter. The group hadn't the money to go out and find a real cancer victim and photograph him, and Terry happened to be available. The literature went on to say: "Delays in the testing and utilization of new scientific discoveries are today's most serious impediment to the eradication of cancer. Peyton Rous, for example, made the landmark discovery in 1911 that certain kinds of cancers could be transmitted through viruses. It took more than half a century for that discovery to be taken seriously—and did not occur until the scientist was eighty-six years old! Alexander Fleming discovered penicillin in 1928. It was fifteen years before his discovery was acknowledged and put to use! In the interim, many people died needlessly from infection.

"Vested interests, the jealousy of other scientists, bureaucratic inefficiency, the simple ingrained hostility of Establishment authorities to new ideas—all are obstacles that delay use of a new development or suppress it indefinitely.

"Citizens' Campaign has been organized because such obstructions are unacceptable to victims of cancer whose only hope is an early scientific breakthrough—and unacceptable to the rest of us who live in fear of the disease. The Campaign has therefore arisen as a grass roots movement to search out the new ideas wherever they exist and rush financial support for their development to the laboratory bench. In this way promising discoveries can be brought to the public aid as rapidly as possible. CCNAC is further founded on the belief that unless the people do it themselves, cancer will never be eradicated."

The brochure then outlined its goals: "Put out an international dragnet for NEW idea to combat cancer, and rush support to the proper laboratories so evaluation of those new ideas can commence immediately.

"Eliminate the interminable delay between the making of a discovery in the laboratory and conversion to public use.

"Support research on means of preventing cancer as well as treating it—for example, by providing funds for serious investigation of the effectiveness of anti-cancer nutritional supplements.

"See to it that the bulk of money raised gets to the researcher.

"Publish a newsletter communicating the latest advances against cancer so that members may be well informed should the disease strike.

"Provide an information service to direct members to the best centers, here and abroad, for treating the particular form of the disease afflicting members or their loved ones."

To spread this message and round up veritable carloads of dollars to wipe out cancer, Terry became a traveling evangelist. "I gave several radio interviews. I went to talk before the Rotary. I spoke in front of a blind group. We had a Betamax and a TV and some tapes. My cousin and I used to go out to flea markets and spread the word about Raymond Damadian and his fantastic cancer machine all over Long Island. I went to church groups. I went to American Cancer Society groups, even though he had been turned down five times or ten times by them. In the flea markets, we had a big glass container where people could shove money. I can remember standing out in the rain at a flea market under a canvas tent preaching NMR. By the way, I should make it clear that I'm not a scientist. I took biology twice because I flunked it the first time. I was not talking from loads of firsthand knowledge. We went into parades. Danny Culver, my cousin, and I built a float for the St. Patrick's Day parade, a big deal out in Westhampton. It was this big green shamrock with CCNAC and our slogan on it. It was hard work. It was fun. Some of it was embarrassing. There were all these doctors telling us what jerks we were. But we did it because it was a lot of fun and because we believed NMR would totally eradicate cancer someday and out of love for Raymond. And we did it for long, long hours. I tell you, it was almost cause for divorce."

Rather than in carloads, the money trickled in in dribs and drabs. Over several years, the total would never exceed a figure in the low five figures. Terry recalled, "My father threw in a thousand here and there, my uncle threw in a thousand.

My God, Damadian really needed the money. To pay Minkoff and Goldsmith. The magnet cost a lot of money to run. I was in charge of paying all the bills and keeping the books. Every dime that ever came in was used. Over a weekend at a flea market, for twenty-four hours of work, we'd bring in a hundred dollars or two hundred dollars for our efforts. That paid another salary for a week. That bought gas. Raymond would call up and say, 'How much money have we got?' And I'd say, 'It's pretty low, maybe a hundred bucks.' 'Well, any more coming in?' I'd say I didn't know. I remember one time we were down to twenty-five dollars. But somehow, some way, more money would come in. A friend would send something in or someone would die. Death helped. We had a program where you could contribute money to the cause in memory of a loved one. So we'd go and do a memorial service and raise five hundred dollars or something like that. Sometimes we'd go to a flea market and come back with fifty dollars. Little kids would toss in quarters. Pocket change from little kids that might have gone for bubble gum or Tootsie Rolls was paying the guys in the labs, making this thing happen."

SEVEN

On February 5, 1974, Raymond Damadian was issued United States Patent No. 3,789,832 covering his invention "Apparatus and Method for Detecting Cancer in Tissue."

Also, in 1974, largely in response to strong and spirited lobbying by Kenneth Olson, the head of the National Cancer Institute's diagnostic branch of the Division of Cancer Biology and Diagnosis, the NCI awarded a contract to finance three scientists in a thoroughgoing study of the application of NMR for cancer detection. The contract spanned two years. Something like sixteen scientists applied for the money, and after the bids had been duly considered, Raymond Damadian received a hundred thousand dollars a year, Donald Hollis at Johns Hopkins University seventy-five thousand dollars a year, and Carlton Hazlewood at the Baylor College of Medicine fifty thousand dollars a year. The researchers were expected to experiment with human tissue samples in malignant, benign, and normal states in an attempt to determine just how dependable NMR signals were in differentiating the conditions. Though Damadian took a dim view of being lumped with two other scientists under the contract when he felt that rightfully he should be funded alone to pursue his discovery, he was jubilant that he now had a healthy lump of money to work with. Before it was exhausted, he felt sure he would prove to the scientific community the grand promise of his development.

Just getting samples to study, however, proved to be an immediate and rather complicated difficulty for Damadian. It was necessary to cajole pathologists and surgeons to cooperate by saving fresh biopsy samples from the operating rooms. Damadian needed them before they had been put on ice or dunked in formaldehyde. Although University Hospital was a convenient and obvious source for samples, Damadian had never enjoyed much success in enlisting the hospital's support. As Ken Zaner, one of the graduate students who worked in the lab, said, "We couldn't get any cooperation from our own institution to get samples from the pathology department. I think it was the magnets. There was something peculiar to scientists about using magnets. As soon as we mentioned magnets around dinner at the cafeteria, there would be this chuckling. It was kind of weird. It was like we were doing voodoo or baying at the moon."

Thus Damadian found it necessary to hire a taxi and dispatch one of his graduate students to either Memorial Hospital, which was nearby, or to the Sloan-Kettering Memorial Cancer Center in Manhattan. The student would scoop up four or five specimens at a shot, stash them in a bucket, and rush them back to Downstate. This would continue day after day, for Damadian felt impelled to work longer and longer hours and he was insistent that there always be samples to test. Zaner, who often found himself the tissue envoy, says, "Damadian's favorite quote was, 'Don't tell me it can't be done, just do it.' He pushed everyone pretty hard. I used to come in around eight, then seven, then six-thirty. We would sometimes get a critical glance from him if we left at ten o'clock. He was often there until midnight." Over the two-year period, Damadian buried himself in the tissue work. Goldsmith was assigned the immediate direction of the project, and he found several technicians whom he trained. Before they were through, they would run tests on more than a thousand human tissue samples.

At one point, soon after the NCI contract was awarded, a conference was held for all of the scientists working under

NIH grants, some two hundred individuals. One person representing each project was chosen by the NIH to deliver a lecture on the state of the work. Damadian, naturally enough, expected to be chosen to speak about NMR. Instead, Donald Hollis was picked. "I was sitting in the audience," Damadian has said of the occasion, "listening to somebody else talking about my discovery. All he did was copy me. I almost went crazy. I couldn't stand it. I remember that as the most outrageous thing to happen to me up to that time. I was under the impression that you discover something and you get credit for it. I sat in the audience in a rage. I remember somebody coming up to me afterward and saying, 'Hey, Raymond, that was your discovery. Why didn't you give the lecture?' I was learning fast the ugly rules of the game."

During the course of the contract, the three scientists were coming to entirely different conclusions, and their enthusiasms rose to different levels. Damadian was a fervent believer. He was finding some overlap between malignant and benign tumors using T1 studies, but he and his students (credit must be given to Jason Koutcher in particular) worked up a combination of T1 and T2 readings that was turned into what was called a "malignancy index" that seemed to separate the tumors adequately. Hazlewood was confident that the NMR signals differentiated malignant from normal tissue, but he was running into problems with malignant and benign samples. "We had a lot of overlap on our data," he says. "It puzzled me. I didn't understand why."

Hollis's perspective was at the other extreme from Damadian's. He was decidedly pessimistic, and his sour attitude fed the already well-formed suspicions of the NCI review people. Hazlewood, sensing ominous warnings of what lay ahead, got nervous. "I could tell from listening to the damned bureaucrats that they were going to cut off our funds after two years. So I shifted my emphasis back to investigating the fundamental mechanism of the cell that was giving rise to the differences in relaxation times in normal and malignant tissue. The bureaucrats were getting scared to death that they were wasting their money. At one meeting, Hollis said that the idea of scanning the human body was visionary nonsense, and everyone clapped. They were really bad times. They wanted us to do as good as the pathologists, but the pathologists had had a hundred years and we had had less than a decade."

Damadian went on observing, noting, calculating, recording. He felt convinced that Hollis's conclusions were based on faulty research; a notable weakness, he said, was Hollis's use of normal tissue in the bodies of sick people as control tissue. In one experiment, Damadian's lab showed that normal tissue extracted from a diseased organ, even if it originates some distance away from the tumor, has abnormal NMR characteristics.

The next few months for Damadian, however, were perfectly miserable. Near the completion of the contract, Hollis, Hazlewood, and Damadian convened in Bethesda, Maryland, to discuss their progress with NCI officials. Hazlewood again reported that he was hopeful, especially in the detection of breast cancer. "I told them that I felt NMR was useful in complementing the pathologist in the detection of cancer and the classification of cancer." Damadian, of course, was brimming with confidence and expressed his anxiety to proceed to more ambitious studies. Using the malignancy index, he claimed that he could discriminate, with satisfactory reliability, between normal tissue and tumors of the breast, spleen, skin, and lymph. Hollis, though, remained the unyielding Doubting Thomas. Hearing his flat pronouncements that further research along these lines was leading to a barren destination—in short, it was all a scientific wild goose chase—Damadian stared at him with hostility. Before Hollis could complete his remarks, Damadian, who had grown rosy with indignation, swung around to Hollis and shouted at him, "You're setting back science by ten years. If you don't believe in this, you ought to get out of the field."

Hollis, showing his own blistery side, burst out, equally emphatically, "I like this field and I'll get out of it when I feel like it."

A committee was required now to review the work and either recommend or not recommend continuation of the contract. Four investigators—two physicists, a chemist, and a pathologist—filed opinions, which were summarized in a final report by the group's chairman, Dr. Edwin Becker. On the whole, the reports of the committee members were extremely positive about Damadian's experiments. For example, one member wrote, "I would recommend that this contract be either renewed or extended for an additional period of time. . . ." A second member declared, "It would be a crime for the Diagnostic Branch to stop support at this time after being quite forward-looking in supporting a contract in this area two years ago. There were problems with that contract and, in some sense, the idea of NMR for cancer detection was 'oversold' . . . there are many problems to overcome in instrument design as well as in measurements in order to establish this technique. Nonetheless, this technique appears to this reviewer to have great potential, particularly for screening, and it would be quite premature for the Diagnostic Branch to drop support at this time." Becker's report was less sanguine. At one point, he wrote, "Further development of NMR imaging is, I think, a very worthwhile objective, possibly for cancer detection as well as for other practical medical applications. Damadian started late, and his results so far are not very impressive. I personally believe that his approach is less likely to be successful and efficient than those already being developed elsewhere, but he may move ahead rapidly. I would favor his continuing this development work for another year or so, but I can't see why his work should be funded by the Diagnostic Branch in preference to that by Lauterbur and others." Despite the positive language of the other reviewers, Becker, in summarizing the conclusions of the committee, essentially reiterated his own feelings. He wrote: ". . . Damadian's study of non-proton NMR should not be supported by DB. Damadian's development of imaging techniques should continue, but whether with DB support is questionable."

As the expiration date of the contract drew close, renewal seemed unlikely. Ken Olson, its biggest champion, was gone from the NCI and had been replaced as the head of the diagnostics review committee by Dr. Edward Pomerance. Damadian took an opportunity to visit him and was bluntly told that the contract probably wouldn't be renewed, a prophecy that soon came true.

When he was officially informed of this, Damadian flew into a violent rage and, as he had done on several occasions in the past, appealed to his Queens congressman, Joseph Addabbo, who lent a sympathetic ear. Addabbo promptly assigned an attorney, Irving Maness, to tackle the Damadian case. Among other things, a meeting was arranged with the head of the National Cancer Institute. Damadian temporarily got an additional $25,000. He pleaded for more. He was told that he would receive a year's extension and be funded with $150,000, but before the money was formally approved the anti-NMR factions in the NCI regained the upper hand and the extension was abruptly canceled. In a barely controlled fury, Damadian made a phone call one night to the home of an official high up the ladder at the NIH. "I asked him how he could do this to me. He said, 'Dr. Damadian, I'm playing Chinese checkers with my daughter. I do not wish to be disturbed. Goodbye.' What I wanted to say but didn't was, 'Excuse me, but is that daughter of yours immune to cancer?'

He's busy playing Chinese checkers! Does he think he can't get the disease? I used to go around and ask people, 'Are you immune to the disease?'

"The second force besides the established NMR community," Damadian says, "was the cancer establishment. They didn't want this machine to happen. It might get rid of the disease. That's why we still have cancer with us. Notwithstanding Richard Nixon, who put one billion dollars into cancer each year for three years, the only thing we've got out of this expensive cancer research is that deaths from cancer keep going up."

He was sitting in a diner, finishing up a late lunch, and he twirled a ballpoint pen around his index finger as if it were a baton. "The cancer community is the worst. It would break your heart to know the truth. The vested interests in this business are decades-deep, maybe centuries-deep. The cancer industry may spend forty-five billion dollars a year. The sad truth is that more people are living from cancer than dying from it."

Damadian never managed to cultivate many sympathetic supporters at the NCI. The one man who did invest considerable energy in trying to round up money for him was Kenneth Olson. Olson worked part-time and full-time for the NIH for a number of years, starting in the early 1970s. He is now retired and lives in Florida, where I spoke with him one afternoon. Olson is a blunt, tough-talking man, fun to spend time with. Listening to him, the minutes fly. He is never too shy to express his opinions, however many feathers they may ruffle. In that respect, he is much like Damadian.

"We had a committee that reviewed grant applications," he said, "and I presented this idea of Damadian's and the committee said, 'We'll quietly bury this.' I was just infuriated. What were they doing? I said that if Roentgen walked in that day saying he could see bones in the body with a machine, they'd laugh him out of the room. I'm afraid that didn't make much of an impression on my supposedly esteemed colleagues." He added, "On the committee, there was only one other person, a man named John Doppman, who said, 'We will look pretty silly if this really develops into something.' I suppose there are quite a few people who are feeling silly today."

He continued, "Damadian came down and talked to the group at one point. Some of the physicists were skeptical. Others said we should proceed. Hollis was the most antagonistic. The majority said no and for him to apply to the research grants division. He had already been turned down there. They knew damned well that he wouldn't get much there. That was as good as saying, 'Get the hell out of here.' You really can't get over a new idea at the NCI. They want something that will have an application. That's what they're used to.

"My feeling about this is that research should be ninety-nine percent worthless. You shouldn't have an answer. You shouldn't have an answer that this is going to cure dandruff or turn carrot juice into a propellant when you're doing basic research. I can't explain it, but I think people are a little bit reluctant to give public money to abhorrent people or crackpots. They don't understand something: Crackpots come up with some of the best ideas. I thought what Damadian had was one of the few new ideas to come up before the institute. I thought it should be pursued to the hilt. But everyone else was afraid it was going to be a dud and it would reflect badly on the department."

When I asked Olson why Damadian seemed to have such difficulty with the NCI, he quickly replied, "Do you know Damadian? I like him very much, but he is vitriolic, and if people don't understand him right away he thinks the people are stupid. He hits the roof. Many times I had to hold the receiver away from my ear when he called at the NCI and I had to calm him down before we could get on to any sort of productive conversation. In short, the man had a temper."

Then he said: "I think there was a certain amount of pettiness. He brought in a congressman at one point, and they didn't like that. He had patented his machine, and the NCI doesn't like things that are patented. Also, physicists had this for years and didn't come up with the idea, and Damadian was a physician and he came in and discovered it. The physicists missed the boat. Nobody likes to miss the boat. If you missed the boat, you weren't likely to cheer for the guy who made it."

I asked Olson if he ever suspected that there might have been any sort of conspiracy to do Damadian in.

"No," he replied, "I don't think there was any conspiracy or anything by the members of the committee. They just thought Damadian was a crazy physician or a wild-eyed scientist who claimed too much for what he had."

Realizing that it might be difficult in retrospect to tell a wild-eyed scientist from a man with a stroke of genius, I asked Olson if the committee might indeed have made a responsible judgment.

He answered straight back, "No, I don't think it did. When you get a bunch of people on a committee, there's sort of a herd instinct. Three or four are kind of down on a project and they're eminent in their field and so the others who know less about it tend to take the opinion of these dominant people rather than think on their own. Damadian would call us and harangue us. He did that to me and to others. I believe that as professionals, we should have seen through the kook in Damadian. I didn't care if he was crazy as a hoot. He did what we asked him to do. The evidence was there. It was our job to support him. I've been a teacher. I've had wild-eyed students. It was my job to find a place for them and encourage them."

Olson was just about talked out by now. Before we concluded our conversation, though, he threw in an additional thought: "Grantsmanship and contracts are an art. We would get these beautiful glazed applications from Yale and Harvard and they were beautifully and succinctly written and that impressed people. A committee is very impressed by smooth operators, even if they don't do a damned thing. These people would come in and they were really suave and had lovely presentations and they snowed people. To give money to some ordinary mortal who was way out—why, forget it! Downstate is a fine institution, but it doesn't have the reputation of a Harvard or a University of Chicago for physics. To give money to a physician from Downstate seemed way out. Someone who's a maverick has trouble getting money. They're the crackpots of the world. They often do the best work."

The breeze blowing from other laboratories at Downstate was getting frostier for Damadian as well. As Ken Zaner once noted, "At first, with the water stuff, the other people at the university thought Damadian was a little bit of a crackpot. Then, when he went on to the NMR work and talked about scanning humans, they thought he had cracked up completely." It was more than just Damadian, though. He seemed to attract—and tolerate—rather unusual laboratory companions. "It was a pretty strange crew all around," Zaner said. "Mike was certainly different. I was sort of a flake. There were people who would drift in and out of the lab who would not have the slightest problem passing as escapees from mental institutions."

For a period of time, an electrical engineer was hired as a consultant to develop an experimental antenna and to work on an amplifier. He quickly became known for the peculiar stories he would tell. Once he started ruminating about an assistant who used to work for him, who he said liked to have sex with lizards. The man claimed that he went through a couple of pet lizards a month. One day, according to the engineer, the assistant dug out a picture of a dinosaur from his wallet and proudly announced that that was his wife. What bothered the others in the lab was the fact that the engineer told this story with a completely straight face. They weren't sure if he actually believed it or not.

At another point, Damadian was approached by an elderly Manhattan gynecologist named Sheldon McLean. He claimed to be successfully treating people suffering from cancerous tumors by exposing them to pulsating magnetic fields. He had constructed a sizable magnet with a four-thousand-gauss field that would be directed at the tumor and then flicked on and off. Though he insisted with some force that the cure worked, he admitted that he couldn't prove it scientifically. Colleagues were ridiculing him, and he was unable to find laboratory space to conduct proper experiments to validate his treatment. There was a confidence and certainty to his manner. In mulling it over, Damadian thought it possible that McLean was onto something, though exactly what he was onto was anybody's guess. In any event, he was curious about anything having to do with magnets and cancer, and thus he invited McLean to work in a spare corner of the lab.

McLean was in his seventies. Very distinguished-looking. Hollow-faced, with alley-cat eyes. Despite his age, his brown hair was free of even a trace of gray. He told Damadian that his magnet had turned his white hair brown. He arrived with an assistant who might easily have been mistaken for a longshoreman. He had close-cropped gray hair, a couple of teeth missing, tattoos on his arm. They brought with them a fairly sizable electromagnet that worked with a carousel designed to hold rats. The carousel would twirl around beneath the magnet, pausing to allow a rat to be zapped by the magnetic field. "We thought, hey, it's a little crazy, but let's give it a try," Ken Zaner said.

McLean proved to be an unreliable experimenter. He would show up one day, then not appear again for several weeks. The better Damadian got to know him, the more suspicious of the man he became. McLean told Damadian that he regularly stuck his own head in his magnet because he found that the magnetic field was increasing the energy flow into his body. Damadian thought that that was an awfully dangerous thing to do and became convinced that the man had screwed up his head. "When you talked to him, he was unable to complete a coherent sentence," Damadian said. "You'd be sure he was cuckoo if you met him. I figured the magnet was doing this to him. It's a creepy thing, putting your head in a magnet like that."

The others in the lab were getting wary of him as well. Zaner remembered, "I tried to strike up a conversation with the guy one day and I realized he was really from Mars. The final proof that he was around the bend was when my girlfriend, who was a graduate student in biochemistry, came in one evening to meet me for dinner. While she was waiting for me, he cornered her and said, 'You know, the famines are coming.' 'What?' she said. He said, 'The famines are coming, but don't worry, the electromagnets will turn electromagnetic energy into food energy.' That's when I realized that he wasn't an eccentric genius."

McLean, encountering ruinous difficulties with his experiments, eventually grew impatient and disgusted and gathered up his magnet one day and hastened from the lab. "We were mavericks, and so when you have a novel idea, the whole world tells you you're crazy and you begin to wonder if the world is crazy," Zaner said. "So we had an open mind to odd people. It just happens that sometimes the world is right."

A certain gravity and inner gloom had been forced on Damadian by the increasing hostility to his views, but he found a constant source of encouragement in Cope. Although a skeptic himself at first, once Damadian had shown with his experiments the splendid promise of NMR in medicine, Cope became an unflagging cheerleader. These people are narrow-minded fools, Cope would remind him. Ignore them. Kindled by this, Damadian proceeded to buy a magnet that could scan a live mouse. By February 1976, he succeeded in focusing the NMR signal using his FONAR method. This meant that he could move the signal systematically throughout the interior of a live animal to produce a scan.

He began experimentation with a subject which he officially called Pioneer Mouse. He anesthetized it and slipped a small coil around its chest. As he was trying to get a proper focus, however, Damadian was turning the dial and putting more and more current into the coil, and before he caught himself, he found that Pioneer Mouse was fried. "I cooked him. It was a screw-up on my part. I just fouled up."

Enter Pioneer Mouse No. 2. On March 11, while Damadian was busy with other things, Minkoff obtained an extremely crude image of a tumor in the anterior chest wall of the mouse. For four hours, the mouse remained in the coil, signals being read from its chest. The image, reconstructed by computer, looked rather like a hazy, multicolored Christmas-tree ball. The tumor, an Ehrlich ascites solid neoplasm, showed up as an orange-pink and red region at the very bottom of the image. In a normal mouse, the thoracic region would be blue. When it came time to publish the results, Damadian made Pioneer Mouse No. 2 the coauthor of one of the papers. The image was submitted to *Science* magazine and eventually appeared on the cover of the December 24, 1976, issue. Larry Minkoff was subsequently told by a *Science* editor that the magazine was looking for something appropriate for Christmas for the cover and the mouse image had the unmistakable look of a Christmas ornament.

By now, Damadian had no doubts about the explosive potential of NMR scanning. He knew that it would open a window into the human body sharper and more revealing than any detector of disease yet invented. When Wilhelm Conrad Roentgen discovered the X-ray in 1895, he opened the very first window into the living body. But it has always been a blurry window. An X-ray picture offers little sense of depth, and while bones show up quite distinctly, many of the softer tissues appear as mere shadows in shades of gray. With X-rays, different parts of the body allow varying amounts of the X-radiation to reach the film. Based on the differences, radiologists can discriminate between organs, other tissue, and bone. But since most pathological lesions and normal tissues have similar X-ray absorption properties, the resulting images are simply a reflection of gross anatomical size and shape and don't discriminate between normal and abnormal tissue. Thus lesions can go undetected unless they become large enough to actually change the shape or size of the organ.

In 1970, Godfrey Newbold Hounsfield, an electronics engineer at the British company EMI (which was best known, through its record division, for promoting the Beatles), and Allan MacLeod Cormack, a physicist at Tufts University in Medford, Massachusetts, wiped some of the haze off the window when they invented an X-ray machine that employed a computer to fashion clear, cross-sectional views of the body. Their development of computerized axial tomography, commonly referred to as CAT scanning, enabled doctors to see far crisper images of the interior of the body, and their achievement eventually won them the Nobel Prize in physiology or medicine in 1979. The two researchers had never met and had conducted their research independently of each other. The CAT scanner rapidly rotates a single X-ray beam around a human head or torso. The data it accumulates are then assembled by a computer into cross-sectional pictures, free of the obliterating shadows that mar conventional X-ray images. The technique quickly proved especially useful in detecting brain tumors. CAT scanning, however, is also hobbled by limitations. Bone obstructs a CAT scan. While the images furnish anatomical information, they relay little about the health of the body's organs. Look at a CAT scan and, in fact, you can't tell if a patient is alive or has been dead for several days.

NMR scanning, Damadian believed, would expose the internal landscape as never before. An NMR machine could see with clarity through the thickest of bones. Unlike the other windows, it could produce chemical information. It emitted no harmful radiation. What more, Damadian wondered, could medicine ask for?

Damadian next ordered, from a company called Canada Superconducting, a magnet that was large enough to contain a monkey. It was a brooding six-foot-high presence that somehow seemed out of place in the laboratory. Once the new machine was in working order, a bush baby was acquired, and Damadian was soon engrossed in trying to produce an image of it. Keeping the monkey quiet in the device, however, was a nettlesome problem. Such was the design of the magnet that when the monkey was shoved inside to be scanned, the beast completely vanished from sight. One day, Minkoff was trying to get readings from the monkey when all of a sudden the signal disappeared. Oh, no, Minkoff thought, something's wrong with the equipment. For two hours, he hunted through the electronics, looking for the problem. Exasperated, he finally took a peek inside the magnet. Fully awake now, the monkey had extracted itself from the coil and was squatting at the top of the probe, arms folded across its chest, gazing at Minkoff as if he were an idiot. Minkoff eventually got several crude images of the bush baby, but they were never published.

By now, however, Damadian was antsy. As far as he was concerned, an adequate amount of experimentation had been done with animals, adequate at least for him. All of the pieces of the jigsaw seemed to be coming together. He could think of one thing only: to accelerate his work and move on to something bigger and grander, something that, with luck, would still his critics.

EIGHT

He was standing in the lab, parceling out the assignments. He made the situation clear. There was not enough money— not nearly enough money—to buy a magnet that would be big enough to accommodate a human being. So they would have to build it themselves from scratch. Damadian ran his gaze slowly across their faces. It was April 1976.

Weighing the merits and faults of the group, but mostly pulling a number out of the air, he suggested that the team might be able to build a machine in six months. One of his favorite comments, however, was, "I always tended to underestimate how long it would take to do something by a factor of two."

It was an especially dark time to be starting such a remarkably time-consuming and forbidding project. The pulse of the lab was far from strong. Morale, which tended to follow a roller-coaster trajectory, had sunk to one of its lowest points. Everyone was bummed out about the cancellation of the NCI contract. Influential scientists like Hollis were calling the entire idea preposterous. The joke making the rounds of the scientific community when the notion of a human-sized NMR machine was brought up was "Well, how fast are you going to spin the patient?" When a test-tube sample was inserted in a conventional NMR machine, the test tube would be spun at something like a hundred rotations a minute in order to create a more homogeneous sample and thus generate a stronger signal. So scientists imagined putting a patient in a mammoth machine and then having him whirled around as if on a carnival ride, and the vision consistently drew gales of laughter.

On any number of occasions, Damadian would deliver a lecture somewhere and when it came time to accept questions a chemist would inevitably stand up, clear his throat, and say, "Uh, Dr. Damadian, would you mind telling the audience how fast you plan to spin the patient?" And then the laughter would erupt.

There were others, nonetheless, who were chasing Damadian's dream with something approaching, if never quite equaling, his intensity. The grapevine from competing laboratories was humming with discomforting suggestions that he was falling a step or two behind. Paul Lauterbur was deep into his own research. The first NMR image Damadian had ever seen was one that Lauterbur had shown him a few years before. It was an image of the chest of a healthy mouse. ("I think he showed it to me to impress me. I was impressed.") Also active in the hunt were two groups in the physics department at the University of Nottingham, one led by the determined Peter Mansfield and another headed by Waldo Hinshaw and E. Raymond Andrew, whose exposure to NMR went back to his work in 1948 as a postdoctoral fellow at Harvard with Edward Purcell. Nottingham had seen a significant amount of research into NMR. Around 1970, the university undertook a project from the Ministry of Defense to study information storage with NMR field gradients. The attention of the researchers there was drawn to the clinical possibilities of NMR by chance events. Andrew, who was the chairman of the physics department, and Hinshaw had been at a conference in Bombay, listening to a speech by Lauterbur on NMR imaging. At that point, neither was aware of the papers of either Damadian or Lauterbur. This seems interesting, they thought, though, as Andrew recalled, "It was felt that Professor Lauterbur's technique was perhaps too complicated." On the lengthy plane ride back to London, Hinshaw fooled around with some ideas on a piece of paper, and by the time his plane landed he had conceived an imaging technique of his own. His approach was to use oscillating gradients to isolate a point, line, or plane in space; in effect, he was able to focus on a desired area by wiping out the signals from all other parts of the sample. It would be some time later, however, before he would achieve good images with the method, not until December 1977, in fact, at which time he showed nice images of a lemon and a human wrist. In 1974, Mansfield thought up a method by which he would selectively excite NMR signals from a particular segment of the sample as a way to home in on a desired slice. He did some images of dead chicken legs, then in 1974 tried a human index finger, which wasn't very successful. He attempted a finger once again in 1975 that resulted in a far better picture—he was amazed by the amount of detail—and he published his report in the British *Journal of Radiology* in March 1976. He had ordered a resistive magnet large enough to contain a human body, in which his interests would stretch in ever-widening circles; he would move on to study live rabbits, rats, guinea pigs, a cat, and a human cadaver ("I remember carrying a cadaver torso and putting it in the machine. It makes me cringe to think of it now"), and finally to experiment with himself. "Over in England, everyone was thinking then that clinical applications were the most important thing," Andrew said.

Yet another group, headed by John Mallard, in the department of biomedical physics and bioengineering at the University of Aberdeen in Scotland, was very much in the race. What's more, EMI, the British firm responsible for the introduction of CAT scanning, had set up a research program in NMR imaging. Scientists Hugh Clow and Ian Young were assigned to the project, and EMI ultimately undertook an effort under the code name Neptune to develop a whole-body scanner.

All of these experimenters were flush, and Damadian

wasn't. As Damadian's fortunes melted, theirs seemed to co-agulate. Damadian feared that if he didn't produce a human image there was no chance that he'd ever get any credit for fathering the field. He worried most of all that Lauterbur, once the final hand was played, was going to win all the chips.

When he considered the competition, Damadian thought the odds were at best fifty-fifty that the first human scan would be achieved at Downstate. "To be honest, I didn't really think we were going to beat the others," he confided later. "But I thought we had a chance of winning. A chance. I was doubtful that Lauterbur had the capability to do it, though Mike would keep telling me, 'Don't underestimate Lauterbur. He's got postdocs over there. Maybe one of them can do it.' I was sure that the British had the capability to do it." But the force driving Damadian was his intense hatred of Lauterbur. "What used to get me upset was when I traveled around to meetings and everyone was talking about zeug-matography and I wasn't getting mentioned at all," Damadian said. "I'd hear this and I would split a gut. I was really in a white heat. I would have died before I let him beat me. There was no way in human possibility that I was going to let Lauter-bur get that image before me. We didn't want to come in second in the race to get the first image of a live human being. We didn't want to fail in being first in the flying machine."

If there was ever doubt in Damadian's mind that others might be seeking to steal credit for his discovery, obliteration of it was never far away. One evening around this time, Damadian took his family to the movies in Forest Hills. One of the attractions was a short documentary dealing with scien-tific events of note. The first transatlantic flight in a balloon was portrayed. There was some coverage of a single-man air-plane that the pilot pedaled. Then the camera panned in on a young woman scientist, identified as working at the Baylor School of Medicine. She was hunched over an oscilloscope, and the narrator explained that she was at work on her exciting and far-reaching new discovery, the application of NMR to detect cancer. Damadian was momentarily stunned, before his mood turned to outrage.

His son Timmy swiveled to face him and said, "I thought that was your discovery, Daddy."

"It was," he replied. "It was."

So, with mixed emotions, they proceeded headlong to build a magnet that could scan a human. To Minkoff, the prospect seemed like an exciting adventure.

Goldsmith made a sour face. He was miffed. He had just finished supervising the work on the human tissue samples, and he was keen to interpret the data and publish a paper, after which he would be more than happy to pitch in and help build the human scanner. Damadian said no, Jason Koutcher would do the paper; he needed Goldsmith now to work on the big magnet.

A bad feeling developed between Goldsmith and Damadian. Goldsmith sternly told Damadian that he was selfish, that he was thinking only about himself and what he wanted and not about the future of his students. Goldsmith was getting anxious about money—most particularly his lack of it. "I had graduated," he said. "I had my Ph.D., and the name of the game was getting those papers out. Financial security was at the back of my mind. I wasn't an M.D. I couldn't go out into private practice. I was married and I was thinking about a family. I wanted the credentials. I felt my future earnings potential was being damaged."

As Damadian saw it, the human scanner was the ultimate carrot, and he wanted his best people working on it. Goldsmith, to his mind, had gotten lazy lately. He was making excuses.

Neither would budge an inch. Finally, exasperated, Goldsmith said he was quitting and stomped out of the lab. He hastily put together a résumé and sent copies out to a couple dozen colleges, looking for a faculty position. Eventually, Damadian and Goldsmith started talking again and they made a deal. Koutcher would write the first paper on the tissue work, but if Goldsmith took on the magnet he could develop a series of follow-up reports when he had a chance.

The heart of the human scanner team, then, was Damadian, Minkoff, and Goldsmith. It seemed imperative that they get along well. But Minkoff and Goldsmith? Get along?

Michael Goldsmith grew up moneyless in the South Bronx, the rambunctious, woolly area of New York now known as Fort Apache, though, as he likes to put it, "they were only building the fort then." It was the 1950s. Goldsmith's father was an elevator operator. His mother worked behind a sewing machine. Life, in every respect, was a struggle. With his parents working long hours, Goldsmith would often hang out on the gritty streets until midnight playing stickball or punchball. The streets would be choked with kids. They were also riddled with violence. He remembers getting robbed at gunpoint when he was eight and thinking that that was a normal event in life. A couple of years later, he was held up at knifepoint. Fearless, he battled back. The fistfights he fell into were too numerous to count. From the time he was five years old, for reasons that have escaped him, he felt galvanized to become a chemist. As he grew increasingly aware of the abject poverty of his family, he daydreamed about starting a business, preferably one with a scientific bent. It became his driving ambition to find the financial security that his parents lacked.

Complicating matters was school. Some students require gentle nudging to get them through their classes. Michael Goldsmith needed someone to ride and whip him like a jockey. He could skip classes, boycott tests without feeling the slightest qualm. When he was in the eighth grade, school officials threatened to flunk him for hurling a garbage can at a teacher. He hated school so much that the thought of spending an extra year caused him to buckle down; in the ninth grade, he was an honor student.

No matter how he was faring in class, he would always read. "I remember walking to the library—a half mile away—and taking out all the books I could. The limit was six, and I would read them all in a weekend. They were mostly science and all fact. Greek mythology was a large interest. So was poetry." But his moods fluctuated. Dreamy-eyed, unpredictable, moody, he got restless one day and dropped out of high school. Going on to college, after all, seemed superfluous. "Getting into college was an achievement in my world. None of my friends went to college. It was not in the scope of my peer group." He took a commercial aptitude test to see what he was fit for; it was suggested that he become a farmer. That seemed like an unpromising way to find security, so he returned to school. He got a degree in chemical technology from New York City Community College, then entered Brooklyn College in 1966, only to be booted out two years later because of poor grades. He recalled, "One semester I got an A in atomic physics and an F in biochemistry. I was always a poor student. It was a problem I had all my life. I was never interested in lecture courses. The whole idea of school bothered me."

Further fouling up Goldsmith's mind was the Vietnam War and the disruptions that the conflict triggered on college campuses. He had discussed starting a company with a couple of his closest friends, who then went off to fight the war, and Goldsmith became confused. "I wasn't a student radical by any means, but it made me question some basic philosophical values of why I was in school. I couldn't function in that structured environment. I needed a more unstructured setting."

Knowing that a formal education was necessary to fulfill his quest for money, Goldsmith plunged on at night at Brooklyn College, working toward his degree. During the day, he cast about for a job that fit somewhere into his field of training. Downstate was geographically convenient, a short bus ride away. He dropped in one day at the personnel office there. As it happened, Raymond Damadian, new on the faculty and without any help, had recently notified the office that he was looking for a technician to do biophysics work. Somewhere in the channels of the personnel office, the information became garbled. When Goldsmith told the personnel functionary of his background, he was told, yes, a Dr. Damadian was looking for someone for his hematology research. That sounded perfect. Expecting to get a job doing blood counts, Goldsmith went off to see Damadian.

Goldsmith is a huge bear of a man, carrying far more weight than his frame was designed for, bespectacled, bearded, with protuberant eyes and an aureole of stringy dark hair. Every so often, a glint comes into his eyes, and he wears a mysterious smile. Damadian, when he greeted Goldsmith, looked at him with circumspection. He was struck by his immense size and wondered if that would be an advantage or a disadvantage. (Years later, when Damadian needed some especially sturdy brackets to support shelving to hold electronic equipment, Goldsmith would derive pleasure from venturing out to hardware stores and asking the clerk on duty for the strongest brackets that the store carried. The clerk would point out what he was certain were the strongest brackets made. Goldsmith would just shake his head and respond, "Why, these aren't anywhere strong enough," and proceed to bend them with his hands.)

Damadian and Goldsmith talked for a brief spell. At one point, Goldsmith spied an advanced textbook on Damadian's shelf called *Physical Chemistry*. He began discussing parts from the book, and Damadian was impressed by his intelligence. Not often did one find students in medical school so conversant in chemistry. Damadian told Goldsmith that he was doing work on the potassium transport properties of bacteria, which surprised him. What about blood counts? Damadian was mystified. Goldsmith explained what the personnel office had told him, and they had a laugh about the screw-up. Though he was careful not to let on as much to Damadian, the subject of potassium transport didn't interest Goldsmith in the slightest. But he wasn't looking for a career, only a temporary job that would enable him to get his degree and then head out into the business world. Though he was the first person Damadian interviewed, Damadian offered him the job, and he took it on the spot. Later, Damadian encouraged him to enroll in the school and get a doctorate. He would flunk his very first course.

Damadian didn't balk at Goldsmith's lackluster academic performance. He had the sense that Goldsmith was capable of brilliance. In his early weeks in his laboratory, like everyone else, Damadian sought only straight-A students to work with him. "I learned after two cases that this was disastrous. I remember one student who had the highest grades in chemistry Brooklyn College had ever given. He came into the laboratory and I expected a real winner. He couldn't do anything. He would do an experiment and at the end of the day he would say, 'What do the data mean?' And then he would say, 'What do we do next?' Never an idea of his own. Never a thought. So I decided that something wasn't right about straight-A students. Great for getting into medical school but lousy for functioning in the laboratory."

Damadian set Goldsmith to work studying the question of

when the cell increased or decreased its affinity for potassium. At once, Goldsmith proved a capable and industrious worker, and it was only a matter of months before he was promoted to research associate. The longer Goldsmith worked with Damadian, the more the topic of investigation caught his fancy. No longer was it just a job.

As they worked, Damadian and Goldsmith would talk for many hours about Damadian's aspirations. Most days they took their lunch together, and often their dinner as well. Their relationship ripened into a warm bond. "There is no question that he had a profound effect on me," Goldsmith once remarked. "He just infected me with his enthusiasm for the science he was doing, something I was looking for. I was looking for something to get enthusiastic about." On another occasion he said, "Certainly the man is one of the most brilliant men I've ever met, possibly the most brilliant man. From the start, when I first met him, he was interested in curing a major disease. We talked a lot about that. Disease was constantly on his mind. I sensed that there was a need deep inside him to be credited for something great. His philosophy of life seemed to be, 'You're only here once. Do the biggest, most important thing you can.'"

Larry Minkoff is an indubitably cool, laconic individual. He is a delicately built, tousle-haired young man with a pert face and small, sharp eyes. He has a look that is straight as starch. At times, he is easy to talk to. At other times, there is a strong stubborn streak that can take hold of him. When it does, it doesn't take a lot to rankle him. He will work hard, but it helps to walk on his heels. He showed up at Damadian's chaotic Downstate lab one day in 1969 and asked to work with him. Damadian checked him out. Grades? Not at all inspiring, so nothing to worry about there. Minkoff clearly had a creative head on his shoulders. Come in and put on your lab coat.

Science had always seemed to be Minkoff's natural milieu. He once said, "I was interested in science practically from day one. I was always doing science projects that seemed to be a little more complex than the ones that others in my age group were working on." Minkoff was born in 1947 and grew up on Long Island. His father owned his own company, Gift-Pax Incorporated, which distributed packages of sample products—toothpaste, perfume, after-shave lotion—revolving around a theme. There were hospital packs, campus packs, army packs. One of his father's cleverest ideas was to jokingly insert some aspirin into a bridal pack. But he steered his son toward academia. Minkoff's future was also profoundly affected by a horrid family tragedy.

Minkoff had a brother, George, five years older than he, who was stricken by polio as an infant. He wore leg braces and walked with crutches. By the time he was ten, his doctor believed that George might soon be able to get about with the aid of just a cane. At the beginning of that summer, his father drove him to a camp for handicapped children in the Catskills. While they were crossing a narrow and rickety bridge that forded a shallow creek, a truck came barreling down on them from the opposite direction. Minkoff's father whipped the wheel to the right, sending the car hurtling into the creek. He was uninjured, but George's spine was broken. For about seven months he lay encased in a body cast. He went to school by telephone.

Minkoff, being so young, has no recollection of any traumatic effect on him from the crash; after all, he could never remember a time when his brother didn't have braces attached to his legs. "It was not like a brother you used to play ball with and then you can't anymore." When George was removed from the cast, he was put into a body brace that started at his chest and extended to his legs; he wears it to this day. As a result of his restricted mobility, George fastened his attention on intellectual pursuits, most notably science. Once he took keen pleasure in growing tomatoes in a hydroponic, or soilless, system. His interests rubbed off on his younger brother. "He used to make small rockets and shoot them off in the backyard," Minkoff has recalled. "They never seemed to go anywhere, but they made nice explosions." Today, his brother buys and sells rare books and aspires to be a playwright.

As he fiddled with science in his early years, Minkoff began to cultivate a belief that almost anything was possible. This was the age of Sputnik, when the dreams of a lot of American students were rewritten and science and technology became the brass ring. In the early 1960s, there was talk in the American space program of supporting astronauts with oxygen emitted from algae and of possibly using the protein from the algae to feed the astronauts. Such a set-up is known as an ecologically closed system. In 1963, Minkoff built such a system in his basement. In all, he had twenty or thirty liters of algae growing between two fluorescent lights. Inside an airtight fish tank he placed a mouse. For more than a month, he supported the mouse entirely on oxygen from the algae. Two years later, when he was a senior in high school, Minkoff fashioned a device that demonstrated the difference between centrifugal and centripetal force. He attempted to obtain a patent on it, but was informed that a similar apparatus had been thought of before.

After high school, Minkoff enrolled in Worcester Polytechnic Institute in Worcester, Massachusetts, where he studied physics. For his undergraduate thesis, he undertook research on African electric fish. The professor he worked with was habitually attracted to oddities. He once told Minkoff that studying oddities was the most enjoyable part of science. Electric fish were laboratory curiosities that no more than a handful of scientists bothered investigating. Minkoff's specific subject of study was *Gnathonemus peterrii*, the so-called elephant nose. Unlike the familiar electric eel, whose electric force serves as a weapon, the elephant nose possesses an organ that creates an electric field around it that is too faint to serve any defensive function. So what was its purpose? No one knew for sure. The prevailing theory was that the field performed like a radar system, enabling the fish to detect when other fish were swimming nearby. For two years, Minkoff devoted countless hours to prodding the fish with electrodes and feeding them all manner of drugs (sedatives, anticonvulsants) in an effort to get at the root of the mysterious field. Tangling with these fish was not easy. They were smart. "When you tried to play with them, you could never be sure whether it was the experimenter playing with the experimentee or the experimentee playing with the experimenter. For instance, when we would put obstacles in their path they would start playing with the obstacles." In the end, Minkoff amassed a great quantity of data but little hard evidence.

When Minkoff came to Downstate, he had an opportunity to sign on with another professor and continue his study of electric fish. No, he decided. Enough with fish. Meeting with Damadian and talking about his ideas and plans awakened Minkoff's interest in the cell. His reaction upon learning of the sodium-pump theory in medical school was not unlike Damadian's, except he was somewhat less riled by it. "It never bothered me one way or the other, but I figured it was probably wrong. There are a lot of theories in science that are made up more out of necessity than out of status in truth. Unfortunately, a lot of science is people spending their whole lives on a theory that, in five minutes, the technology changes, and a person is proved wrong. What do you tell that person? That his whole life was for nothing?" He wasn't at all worried about trampling on some celebrated egos. "My father was involved in politics in Nassau County. He was a Republican and was always fighting the party machine. He was complaining about petty abuse and so forth. Running against the tide. I once got a threatening phone call at eleven o'clock at night when he wasn't there. I grew up in an atmosphere where if you didn't like the heat you didn't get involved. So when the whole dispute about the pump started, I wasn't bothered so much. I was amused by it. It was kind of funny."

During the early months in the lab, Goldsmith and Minkoff got along reasonably well. They used to drive to Princeton together to eat dinner at a restaurant that Goldsmith liked. They would tinker together on their cars in the Downstate parking lot. Minkoff taught Goldsmith a good deal of physics and electronics. Goldsmith, in turn, tutored Minkoff in bacteriology and chemistry. They shared an important trait: They were both incredibly hard workers. Their energy seemed inexhaustible. Though both were soon to marry, they thought nothing of spending night after night in Damadian's lab.

But as time went on, their capacity for hard labor was about all that they shared. Increasingly, tension began to fill the air. In the best of times, their relationship could be considered frosty. At its worst, it froze solid. Their battles would come to acquire such legendary proportions that it would be said that a picture that Donna Damadian possessed of the two of them standing next to each other with their arms around each other's shoulders and with smiles on their faces was the only moment of cordiality that ever existed between them.

Minkoff never allowed himself to become terribly friendly with anyone in the lab. Another graduate student who knew him said, "Larry had sort of a prince-type attitude. He would dirty his hands on some things, but on others his attitude was that Mike ought to do it." Goldsmith, on the other hand, was an exuberant, captivating person. It was not unusual to come into the lab and see him with his carriage settled into a chair with a cluster of other students bunched around him, like disciples before their guru. He was funny and witty and an intoxicating talker. It sometimes annoyed Damadian and Minkoff that Goldsmith was blithely tending to his flock while they worked. But Damadian put up with it because of Goldsmith's talent and because when he did work, he worked for awesome stretches.

Minkoff was notably less tolerant of Goldsmith. A combative competition developed between them that was at least as intense as the rivalry between the Harvard and Yale football teams. Little provocation was necessary to bring about a showdown. "We had different opinions of things and we didn't back down," Minkoff would say. According to Goldsmith, "It was a personality thing. In many ways, we're opposite personality types and we just get on each other's nerves. We certainly approach things in different ways. We even have different motivations and goals. I'm more philosophical, more thoughtful, less quick to act. You might even say that that's a negative trait. He's more a hands-on guy, who acts, puts things together, and then tries to make them work. My strong motivation from day one was financial security. I don't think Larry had that problem and that motivation."

A streak of impishness ran deep in Goldsmith, and many of the confrontations arose because Goldsmith was fond of tweaking Minkoff simply to get a rise out of him. Sometimes he got more than he bargained for. For a reason Goldsmith no longer remembers, Minkoff once hurled a hammer at Goldsmith. He missed. Goldsmith is hardly a man of violence, though he once came close to punching Minkoff. A piece of equipment that had been delivered to the lab proved to be defective and thus needed to be returned to its manufacturer.

Damadian asked Minkoff to send it back. "He wrapped this thing up and left it in the middle of the floor of the lab," Goldsmith says. "He left it there for the longest time. It must have lain there for two months, and I would trip over it every time I came in. I would say, 'Larry, why don't you get this thing out of here already? It's in everybody's way.' And he would say, 'Yeah, yeah, yeah.' One day, after months of this, I think I tripped over it or something and I said, 'Larry, why don't you get this out of here?' And he said, 'No, why should I get it out of here? Why don't you get it out of here?' I said, 'Why don't I punch you?' And I almost did. He's a funny guy. Sometimes he can be a very ornery person on trivial matters. Sometimes, if you say white, he says black. Very argumentative. I used to have some fun with that. If the guy's going to be predictable, if you know he's going to say black, then you can get him to say all sorts of things."

The lab had a radio that was attached to speakers situated in each of the offices. Certain Saturday evenings, when Minkoff and Goldsmith were cooped up in their respective offices writing papers, Goldsmith would brazenly tune the dial to *Saturday Night Polka Party*. Minkoff would burn up. "Polka music while we were writing papers!" he would exclaim. "It wasn't rock and roll or classical music, something you could live with. It was this polka music. Ugh!"

A classic showdown between the two developed over some worms. Minkoff was storing a batch of sea worms in a tank of salt water for an experiment related to the nervous system. To keep the worms metabolizing slowly, he had put the tank in the Downstate cold room, where the temperature was kept at a chilly 4 degrees centigrade. The worms had been in the tank a protracted period and had died. Some graduate students from down the hall, disgusted with the dead worms, told Minkoff to get rid of them. "They're not dead," Minkoff insisted. The worms were decayed, they were so dead. One graduate student even put a glass stirrer through one of them and the worm never budged as it was sliced in half.

Goldsmith couldn't resist the temptation to play a joke on Minkoff. He took some proteins and poured them into the tank, knowing that the bubbling of the air filter would cause the proteins to foam. He then went to Minkoff and straight-facedly reported that the sea worms were now so far dead that they were decaying and creating a fungus. Minkoff hurried off to the cold room and took a look. A two-inch-high layer of foam sat at the top of the tank, something like meringue on a pie. Then Minkoff returned and announced that no, sorry, the worms weren't dead. This continued for weeks. Each day, Goldsmith added more proteins, until the foam was overflowing the tank. They're not dead, Minkoff kept insisting. Finally, some of the other graduate students declared their intention to kill Minkoff if the worms weren't removed. The death threat produced results. "Larry was just adamant," Goldsmith says. "He was stubborn. It drove me nuts."

When the fights broke out, Damadian was careful not to seem to take sides. He did his best to apply balm to both egos. "It's like raising children. When you have two siblings fighting all the time, interceding can be fatal." Besides, he believed that the competition would have a beneficial effect on their productivity. In this, he was obeying some wisdom that he had picked up from Salvatore Luria, a Nobel Prize biochemist at MIT. Damadian heard him relate a story at a lecture about how when he was stymied by a problem, he put two graduate students on it and he never saw a problem solved faster. The students, he said, would fight with each other over it and work more industriously than they normally might. "Mike and Larry were Damadian's two graduate students," says another student who subsequently joined Damadian's lab. "He loved to play them off against each other. In fact, when Larry and Mike started yelling at each other, Damadian used to laugh and laugh."

A fourth individual had also become quite important in the lab as its computer expert. He was Joel Stutman, a kindly, smiling, gentle man with a narrow face and penetrating gaze. When Damadian first arrived at Downstate, Stutman was a professor in the school's medical computer science program. The son of a Philadelphia pharmacist, he went through his undergraduate years expecting to become a pharmacist himself. While in the service, though, he was exposed to computers and became smitten by them. Problem-solving was always an interest of his, and computers facilitated the exercise.

Soon after Damadian did his first NMR experiments in New Kensington, he approached the chairman of the medical computer science program and asked him if he wished to do some computer work for him. The chairman might have been interested had the request come from someone else. However, he couldn't stand Damadian. He thought he was too pushy. So he told Stutman to go over to Damadian's lab and see what he wanted. Stutman, almost immediately, was captivated by Damadian. "It was obvious he was full of fire. He was full of life. He had a lust for this work that had to be completed. And I have a great deal of respect for someone who will work so hard for an ideal. I had no problem with his personality. I could handle that. Most of the professors at Downstate were afraid of their own shadow and wanted to belong to the same club. If one professor said Damadian was crazy, then they'd all avoid him. And that's how it was. If you were seen with Damadian, well, you might not get promoted to associate professor. He was death. I didn't care about all that. The man was interesting. So if he was death, I'd walk with death."

Thus Stutman started working on problems for Damadian, and, after a bit, he was drawn to what he was doing as never before, if not entirely by choice. "Damadian believes in the statement that the squeakiest wheel gets the most oil. He would complain to you all the time in order to get done what he wanted to get done when he wanted it done. When I came to work for Damadian, I must have had half a dozen other problems that I was working on, and they rapidly went away—they all went away—because Damadian was the only one who cared enough about his research to pound away at me." Most of all, Stutman was looking for interesting work to do, and what Damadian was talking about—building a scanner, taking on cancer—intrigued him. He had a feeble understanding of NMR, enough that when Damadian first told him about his plans for a scanner, Stutman looked slyly at him and commented, "Well, what are you going to do, spin the patient?"

By 1976, the medical computer science program at Downstate had been disbanded, and Stutman had found a job at Hunter College. However, he maintained a consulting arrangement with Damadian. When Damadian decided to begin work on the scanner, he asked Stutman to design a video graphics system that would be able to construct an image from the NMR signals collected by the scanner. Stutman was eager to comply.

Two graduate students, Michael Stanford and Jason Koutcher, were also available to Damadian on a sporadic basis to perform some of the grunt work. "I didn't put any brain work into the project," is how Koutcher has summed up his involvement. "I was one of the horses that ran." Damadian had also hired a full-time machinist, Nean Hu, a young man with a rakish gleam in his eye who was a refugee from mainland China. Hu had had a life marked by hardship and frustration. An avowed hater of communism, he tried to obtain a visa to leave China for thirteen years. For a while, he was suspected of being a spy, and he spent two years in a labor camp. He repaired equipment in the machine shop of a factory, where he learned how to work a lathe and a saw. Though he had gotten a degree in physics, he spoke no English, and so once he finally arrived in America he took a job at an all-girls Catholic high school in Manhattan, tending the boiler and air-conditioning system. By talking incessantly with the girls, he picked up the language. One day he spotted an ad for a machinist in *The New York Times*, answered it, and joined Damadian's lab.

Before anything was built, the Downstate team had to address the problem of space. Damadian had only about five hundred square feet of badly congested laboratory space. Where was he to build a scanner? He went one day to see Calvin Plimpton, the president of the university and one of the constant supporters of Damadian's dream, to plead for additional room. Plimpton said he didn't know where to put him. Damadian suggested the rats' quarters, which were directly across the hall from his fifth-floor lab and were about to be relocated. They consisted of a warren of tiny rooms that had once housed cages of rats that were supplied to biological experimenters. Another professor, as it happened, was also gunning for that space, though he had no particular need for the room. Plimpton managed to convince the other professor to increase his real estate holdings elsewhere and bestowed the rats' quarters on Damadian.

Since Damadian needed open space he had to knock down the walls. Rolling up his sleeves, he expended a good many calories by doing much of the sledgehammer and jackhammer

117

work himself. His students joined in, and several carpenters he knew agreed to moonlight.

When colleagues at Downstate learned of what the Damadian team was up to, the reaction ran from befuddlement to derision. Rostom Bablanian, a professor of microbiology at Downstate who got to know Damadian quite well, has said, "When he spoke about science or he spoke about his machine, it sounded like from out of another world. So people didn't believe him. But these are the fights scientists must make if they are to make advances. Raymond could see more than the average person. He could see that it was possible. He was always different from everyone else. He wanted to teach cell biology, and he approached it from a totally different point of view. Students were just not ready for it. Things like that were what made him look like a madman. He would go on rounds and he would always talk about science, and that turned others off. They weren't interested in science. They were interested in the practical aspects of medicine—what was wrong with somebody. Maybe Raymond didn't understand the ordinary person."

NINE

The human scanner took its first form on paper. The nucleus of the device was a giant magnet. How big a magnet it would take was an unanswerable question. Many people at the time thought a human scan was impossible no matter how large the magnet was. The NMR signal was feeble enough from a test tube. Damadian considered building a resistive magnet, but he was sufficiently unfamiliar with such magnets to fear that he wouldn't be successful. Also, he recognized that it was unfeasible to build a resistive magnet that could enclose a human subject and that was more powerful than one thousand gauss, and he was dubious that that would be strong enough to produce an image. "So I tried to build the most powerful magnet I could dream of building. This could only be possible with superconductivity, so I decided on a five-thousand-gauss superconducting magnet," Damadian says. "I had a few problems, because I had never built a magnet before. Worse than that, I had never built a superconducting magnet before."

If nothing else, Damadian was resourceful. He had a knack for calling up experts and getting them to offer some quick instruction in exchange for nothing but his personal thanks. He was a fast learner. His familiarity with electronics was hazy at best. At one point, he enrolled in the RCA Institute of Electronics to bring himself up to speed. What he learned he taught to his graduate students. To absorb some magnet expertise, Damadian called the physics department at the Brookhaven National Laboratory and was put in touch with the people in charge of magnet building for the nuclear accelerator Isabelle. Glad to help, they gave Damadian a computer program that would enable him to design a magnet.

Damadian experimented with the program and came up with a plan to build a massive superconducting magnet that would consist of two hoops, each two and a half inches thick and fifty-three inches in diameter. The design is known as a Helmholtz pair. Each of the hoops would consist of thirty miles of niobium-titanium superconducting wire, which would have to be tightly and precisely wound around the hoops. Wire of two different diameters was necessary, a total of fifty-two layers, with between seventy-six and ninety-one turns to each layer. If built, the magnet would boast a potential field strength of five thousand gauss and be the ninth-largest in the world. The eight bigger ones all were part of nuclear accelerators, helping to split atoms.

Once the wire was wrapped around the hoops, it would create a solenoid. The same mechanism in your car turns on your ignition. If you use copper wire, you create a resistance solenoid. There are also solenoids made out of superconducting wire. The wire would then be connected to a power source. Superconducting wire conducts electricity with no resistance at all, so you can connect it to a power source and get it to full strength and then disconnect the wire and fuse the leads together and it will continue to conduct electricity forever. In the construction of such a magnet, however, everything must be extremely punctilious. If there are bad parts to the magnet and there are resistive sections in the wire, then the field will weaken eventually. The smallest imperfection in the wire—almost impossible to detect—will cause the field to drift and destroy any image, because the NMR image is exquisitely sensitive. You can't measure imperfections in the wire by ordinary means. You have to try to take images with NMR signals in order to test it. And it is very common to have an imperfection. Damadian once remarked, "I was told when

I first got into NMR that the way to assure good wire was to buy enough to build two magnets and hope that one was good."

Another worry was the risk of keeping a pair of powerful magnets in the same room. Damadian fed the problem into the computer, which ingested it up and calculated that the attractive force between the two magnets would be sixty tons. The power of the force unnerved Damadian, because he feared that the support structure wouldn't be nearly sturdy enough to prevent the magnets from slamming into each other. "If they did, and a patient was in there between them, it would be like being hit by thirty flying Chevrolets." Support structures were constructed by Damadian and Minkoff, and then Minkoff transported them over to the Long Island Testing Lab, which, among other chores, tests the structural capacity of materials for the Long Island Rail Road. The supports did not pull apart. One worry down.

At that point, Damadian was still without materials—in particular the miles of expensive niobium-titanium wire—and didn't have the money to buy them. An act of providence took care of that. "I had a small Westinghouse magnet, and so I called up Steve Lane, the physicist in charge of the superconducting magnet division at Westinghouse, and asked him how to make a superconducting joint. He wanted to know why. I didn't want to tell him I was making a magnet, because he would think I was competing against him. But he persisted, and so I leveled with him. Then he told me that Westinghouse had just thrown in the towel on the superconducting-wire business and had a hundred and fifty thousand feet of superconducting wire. He said I could have it for ten cents a foot. It normally would have cost about a dollar a foot. I needed exactly a hundred and fifty thousand feet. It was like a miracle. So I rented a U-Haul the next day and sent Mike and Larry to Baltimore to fetch it."

Damadian's mother-in-law, Amy Terry, was a devoutly religious person. Through all of his troubles, she would say to him, "Don't worry, we're all praying for you." When he told her about the wire from heaven, she nodded knowingly and said, "You see?" and pointed upward. From then on, whenever there were problems in the lab, the team would decide they'd better get Damadian's mother-in-law back on her knees. Whenever good fortune struck, someone or other would smile and say, "Well, there goes your mother-in-law again."

In the race to be first to scan a human, Damadian was blessed by another, even quirkier stroke of good fortune. Unlike Damadian, Paul Lauterbur was having relatively little trouble raising money to support his research. Funding from the National Institutes of Health allowed him to order a one-thousand-gauss resistive magnet from Walker Scientific, a magnet company in Worcester, Massachusetts, that was more accustomed to building magnets of the sort that scoop up smashed cars in auto graveyards. One morning some months before the Downstate team actually began building their machine, Damadian got a phone call from a friend who glumly announced that Lauterbur had just taken delivery on his human magnet. As he listened, Damadian felt hope ebbing away from him.

"When's he going to do a human?" he asked.

"Well, he can't," the friend chuckled. "He's going to have to get a midget into it. It's too small."

"Oh, how well I remember it," said one of the scientists in Lauterbur's lab. "I unpacked that baby, and when I saw the thing standing there I said to myself, 'Hey, wait a minute, that hole isn't big enough. The damned thing isn't big enough.' I ran and got a tape measure and measured it, and, sure enough, it wasn't big enough. I rushed upstairs and told Paul. He said, 'Oh, come on, of course it's big enough.' I said it wasn't. So he came down and looked and his jaw just about dropped to the floor. Boy, he was ticked off."

"I said, 'Oh, my God,'" Lauterbur recalled. "Incredulity. There were long discussions of whether we should pay or not, and there was a compromise that was eventually worked out. I was shocked. If you bought a new home and tried to go through the front door and it was up to your chin, wouldn't you be shocked?"

Astoundingly, Lauterbur had been foiled by a communications breakdown. According to the specifications he had worked up for Walker Scientific, the magnet was supposed to boast a circular bore of roughly twenty-four inches, inside of which would go an antenna and then inside of that a human being. Walker Scientific, according to Lauterbur, had somehow revised the plans and built the magnet with a sixteen-inch bore without getting his approval. "In the course of negotiations about price and specifications, there were a lot of changes, but the last drawing had the larger bore. In the final talks, they said there would be some negligible changes in the specifications, but they never sent me a drawing. Not until I opened the crate did I see the smaller bore. That was what they considered negligible changes."

Lauterbur has a cartoon thumbtacked to one wall of his basement lab. It shows a newly built canoe, with one end facing upward and one end facing downward. A man sits at a desk with his head in his arms, and he appears to be on the verge of tears. Underneath is scribbled one word: SHIT! Lauterbur said, "This pretty much expressed our feelings when the machine came in."

So Lauterbur hurriedly ordered a larger-bore magnet, while turning the smaller one to lesser aspirations.

"I figured the good Lord had had his way of seeing justice," was Damadian's reaction. "We had a big laugh about it for several days."

Though vastly relieved by Lauterbur's misfortune, Damadian was still full of trepidation. "I didn't know what stunt he might pull next," he said. "I thought he might put a midget in there. That's what I would have done. I would have certainly stuck a midget in that magnet and one way or another got an image."

Goldsmith was put in charge of the effort to wind the magnet. Meanwhile, Damadian and Minkoff would build the dewars that would envelop the magnet and contain the liquid helium and nitrogen that were necessary to cool it. Goldsmith's magnet experience was practically nil. "When I started at this, my knowledge of electronics was such that I could barely light a lightbulb," he said. "It was all seat-of-the-pants learning. We always had the view in the lab that if you're a good scientist you solve your problem wherever it takes you."

To acquire some magnet-building skills, Goldsmith decided to start small and work his way up, and so he built a magnet roughly four inches by two inches to see whether he could make it superconducting. It worked fine. Then he made a larger one, about a foot high and eight inches across, to find out if he could build a magnet that could produce an NMR signal. That worked as well. Next, he wanted to build a third prototype of still larger dimensions, but Damadian nixed the idea. He was getting increasingly panicked that one of the other labs was going to eclipse him, and so he decided to step up the pace.

Goldsmith was none too pleased with the decision, and the reason had to do with welds. No one spool contained thirty miles of wire, the desired length of the winding for each of the big magnets. Goldsmith would be working with spools that contained perhaps a mile of wire apiece. A critical aspect of the magnets, therefore, was the welds that had to be fashioned between the spools with a Kold Weld press to create a wire that was long enough. Needless to say, Goldsmith had never made a Kold Weld in his life. It's achieved by butting the wire ends together and then clamping them in a small press. Niobium-titanium wire forms a strong bond when it is crushed together. Goldsmith practiced making a few welds on the little magnets, but he didn't feel at all proficient at the process. "I was nervous about scaling up from eight inches in diameter to five feet in diameter," he said. "I was worried about the welds not being good. But time was pressing, so we scratched the middle magnet and, at Damadian's insistence, we went on to the human magnet. It would not have been the way I would have done it, that's for sure. But Damadian's not an easy man to talk out of something."

To build the human-sized magnet, Goldsmith first had to fashion a pair of large hoops out of rolled channel bar, aluminum material shaped something like gutters on a house. Damadian and Minkoff drove to Janis Research outside Boston to get the channel bar, and lashed the two gigantic rolls of metal to the car's roof. When they hit the Connecticut border, the water pump on the car broke and they were compelled to spend the night at a motel. The gas station mechanic who fixed the water pump stared quizzically at the big hoops and wondered what in the world they could possibly be for.

To do the machining of the hoops, they had to find a machine shop that had the appropriate-sized lathes. Demand for five-foot hoops was not routine no matter where you were. Goldsmith called on the Brooklyn Navy Yard, which had lathes that were once used to build battleships. They were so immense that railroad tracks served as the beds for the lathes. Goldsmith then needed to fabricate a winding machine to wind the wire with appropriate precision around the hoops, and before that he needed something to serve as a frame for each hoop as it was being wound. Operating on a pinch-penny budget, Damadian and his team prowled through the sub-basement and, like the derelicts you notice sifting through city garbage bins, picked through the debris to find material they could requisition. Damadian was a bold innovator, and when he spied some old metal bookcases of the Erector-set style he knew he had what he needed. Lugged up to the lab, they were configured into a rack for the winding machine.

Weekend after weekend, Damadian, Minkoff, and Goldsmith would also journey to Canal Street, a fount of inexpensive odds and ends near the southern tip of Manhattan, to rummage around in the endless rows of grimy bargain stores in search of additional materials. A lot of the machine tools were purchased along Canal Street at dirt-cheap prices, including an ancient cut-off saw that they got for about $100. Damadian used to ask Nean Hu, the chief proprietor of the saw, "Hey, Nean, how's that saw?" He would grin broadly. It never cut straight. Even the crude machinery he was accustomed to in China was better.

Rooting in bins along Canal Street, Damadian and Goldsmith found several motors, which Goldsmith hooked up to spin the hoop like a Ferris wheel. Minkoff, who was proving to be especially ingenious at building things, constructed a counter to keep track of the revolutions. A small thimble was affixed to the rack with a hole in it so that wire could feed through it. The wire was mounted on a spool. It was then up to Goldsmith, with some help from two graduate students, to wind the magnets. Six days a week, sixteen hours a day, they wound, first one hoop, then the other. By the end of each session, they would be groggy from watching the hoop spin.

Anyone who happened to stroll into Damadian's lab would be baffled as to what manner of scientist worked there. The place had test tubes and flasks, all right, as well as some cages of mice, but it also had torches and welding irons and all this wire and metal. Motors were driving hoops. The team shared the space with roaches that laid eggs in the electronics (since it was toasty warm in there) and thus sporadically caused the computers to fail. The place looked like a machine shop. One faculty member who peeked into the lab around this time remembers arching his eyebrows and thinking, "There is a man who needs a vacation."

Everyone was in the lab seven days a week. The pace was punishing. "Nobody compelled us to put in these hours," Minkoff said. "We were dedicated, probably to the point of insanity."

Meals were eaten whenever it occurred to someone that food might be an interesting diversion. Often the group would simply file down to the university cafeteria and settle for its uninspired offerings. "Eating with Larry and Mike was an experience," Damadian would say. "One would eat nothing and one would eat everything. Moving along a steam table with Mike, he'd say, 'I'll have two of those and four of those and seventeen of those.' And Larry would say, 'I'll have a quarter of that and a tenth of that.' Larry would never even finish the little he would order, so he'd take it back up with him to the lab and it would sit there for days and get moldy and have to be thrown out."

On Sunday evenings, when the cafeteria was closed, a dive of a Chinese restaurant on nearby Church Street was a popular dining choice. Many times they gravitated to Nathan's, home of the "foot-long" hot dog in Coney Island. The place was open until five in the morning, and they frequently worked at the lab until two or three. Also, Goldsmith had a friend who worked at Nathan's and claimed it was the cleanest place he had ever seen. Even though the rest of the neighborhood was sordid and the other early-hour diners were more often devoted to research having to do with alcoholic intake, the place joined the approved list of odd-hour eateries.

It became evident early on that the original timetable for completion of the scanner was going to be radically adjusted. Goldsmith's capriciousness once again became a sore point in the laboratory. He was intensely worried that the human magnet would never work. His nature wouldn't allow him to believe in it. He was scared. Doubt rises quickly in his mind, and he expresses it stubbornly, convincingly. One day, he said to Joel Stutman, in earshot of Minkoff and some of the others, "There will be a human scan done with an NMR machine. But it won't happen here."

"The classic story about Mike," Damadian said, "was when Mike was a graduate student. He did a paper on the Donnan equation, which is a bulwark of physical chemistry. He took Donnan's own data and showed that Donnan was wrong. He wrote up a paper called 'The Invalidity of the Donnan Equation.' It was ironclad. There was no flaw in that paper. He sent it to a biophysical journal. The editor called him up and gave him all sorts of grief about why he was wrong. But Goldsmith was right. And that was a major discovery. Do you know that he wanted to withdraw that paper and strike it out of existence? That paper would not have been published had I not told him he could not withdraw it. Goldsmith was afraid of the heat. People think that science proceeds from a series of objective judgments. That's false. They forget the emotion. The emotion is incredibly important in scientific discoveries. The emotion in Mike told him this wouldn't work."

As his nervousness grew, Goldsmith repeatedly urged Damadian to try doing something less heroic as an intermediate step. Try doing an arm. Take an electromagnet and scan an arm. Then, if all goes well, try the body.

"He kept saying, 'Let's do an arm and let's publish it,'" Damadian said. "I told him I wanted to get to Everest. I didn't want to get halfway up. I wasn't about to go to the

American public and say, 'Hey, ladies and gentlemen, look what we've got. We've got an arm. Look at our arm, ladies and gentlemen.' The whole point of the effort was to do a full body scan. I wasn't about to settle for anything less. Nobody was going to tell me to settle for less."

TEN

It was the hardest work either of them had ever known. Onerous as Goldsmith's job might be, the assignment to build the dewars that Damadian and Minkoff were tackling was far worse. When they took breaks and sat, staring at the disassembled pieces of metal, both men found themselves formidably short-tempered, and they sometimes drifted into a loser's mind-set and wondered if they were up to the task. Each doughnut-shaped dewar was to be ten feet tall, six feet wide, and eighteen inches deep. Each one would weigh one and a half tons. Damadian would later say that had he known how arduous an undertaking it was to build the dewars, he never would have attempted it.

A dewar is a highly sophisticated thermos bottle. It has to keep heat outside, because helium is liquid only at a temperature of at least minus 269 degrees centigrade (absolute zero is minus 273.15 degrees). Were the thermos to warm up to, say, a mere minus 250 degrees, the helium would turn into a gas and, for the purpose of a superconducting magnet, be utterly useless.

A dewar acts to interrupt the three main modes of heat transfer—conduction (heat moving through a solid), convection (heat moving through a gas), and radiation. The dewar design that Damadian followed consisted of a nest of three huge silver doughnuts. The doughnuts were to fit one inside the other. The smallest doughnut, made of stainless steel and polished to a high sheen to act as a shield against radiation, was to contain the magnet and be filled with liquid helium. To take care of conduction, the magnet was designed so that it wouldn't touch any other containers but would be mounted on special supports made out of a material that is a poor heat conductor. The second doughnut was to be filled with liquid nitrogen, which would cool the helium. It was to be made out of aluminum and had to be wrapped with eighty-five layers of super-insulation, thin sheets of aluminized Mylar, that would serve to bounce radiation off it. The last and biggest doughnut was to be a half-inch-thick aluminum vacuum can. When it was assembled, all the air would have to be pumped out of the interior, using a special vacuum working at ten to the minus ninth atmosphere.

The large parts for the dewar were constructed in outside shops. To create the myriad smaller parts, Damadian relied on his Chinese machinist, Nean Hu. His interest in NMR and the possible applications of the technology was negligible. But he proved to be an absolute whiz at machining.

As the dewar pieces came off Hu's workbench, Damadian and Minkoff wrestled with them, trying to get them to fit together. Sometimes they would slip together just right. Often they wouldn't. The rate of work was running at about half what Damadian had originally predicted, and there seemed little likelihood that it would pick up. As one colleague of Damadian's was to say of the effort, "It was sort of like the Egyptians building the pyramids. And it was looking like it was going to take about as long."

Sometimes Damadian and his team slowed down and horsed around, usually when the workload got particularly punishing. Laughing at things, getting mixed up in sophisticated hijinks, were like an injection of some potent narcotic. It drove them on.

Damadian's lab was located in the University Hospital portion of the Downstate complex, which in turn was connected to the Basic Sciences wing. One day, the university decided to lock the door between the two buildings after six in the evening. It was possible to enter the Basic Sciences wing, but not to then return to the hospital side. This posed no problem for most of the faculty members, since it was customary for them to be gone by six. But Damadian's group had need to get into the other wing, which housed the library, the water fountain, and the ice machine—ice was required for the continuing ion-exchange work. Goldsmith and Minkoff were miffed by the new policy and tried to reason with the bureaucracy, to no avail. So, taking justice into their hands, they glued the spring on the door latch shut with metal glue, thus preventing the door from locking. Two days later, the university locksmith repaired it. The next day, Goldsmith and Minkoff glued it shut again, and this time, as a further defense, they filed the screws down so that the locksmith couldn't get the plate off. Muttering through clenched teeth, the locksmith labored for hours and finally put the door back into shape. Undeterred, Goldsmith and Minkoff next welded the lock. Their nemesis, upon seeing the door, went berserk. He had to yank the door off its hinges and haul it to his shop to put it back in working order. This latest offensive triggered a university investigation; the security police were called in and instructed to track down the door deviants.

Hardly shrinking from the challenge, the two came up with a new weapon: a thermochemical fusion device that would melt the latch into a gray blob of goo. Before it could be put into action, a security guard spotted Goldsmith working on the contraption. Damadian received a sharp reprimand from the department chairman. Three weeks later, there was a fire. The locked door was declared a fire hazard and was officially and permanently unlocked.

Goldsmith welded. And Goldsmith wound. And the hoops of wire got thicker and thicker. Winding the hoops, making the joints, took six numbing weeks. As the hours slowly went by, Goldsmith had plenty of time to ponder all the things that could go wrong, and he made good use of the opportunity. "What was on my mind all the time," Goldsmith said, "was that there was no way of testing the wire while we were winding it. What if you wound this thing and then you had a bad piece of wire? The thing would be useless. So I designed it so that all the joints would be fed onto the same switch plate, which could be removed from the dewar for servicing. So if we had a bad wire, I could bypass the wire, and if there was a bad joint, I had enough access to fix it. In those days, it was not at all unusual to have a bad spool of wire. I worried a lot about bad spools of wire."

Goldsmith was by now slipping into depression. Doubts kept assailing him that the machine would ever be constructed. Damadian and he would argue back and forth.

"He was paranoid that people were out to get him," Minkoff said. "The dean was out to get him or this person was out to get him. The president was out to get him. He had this fear of completing a goal. I think he was basically very insecure. He was very talented, but very insecure."

Goldsmith was under extreme pressure, and he did not always react well when the steam was turned up high. Philosophy was his escape valve and had fascinated him since he was young. He was always looking for insights into the purpose of life. "It seemed to me that you reach a plateau every five years or so and you have to gather yourself together and look forward to the next goal. During those plateaus, I would turn to philosophy to get some guidance. What all philosophy books come down to is what other people recognize as the meaning of existence."

Whenever Goldsmith would get depressed, he would vanish into his office or trudge off to the library and, sitting in gloomy silence, would study one of many books on philosophy with which he was familiar. His favorite choice was Kierkegaard's *Fear and Trembling*. His second favorite was the Bible, particularly Ecclesiastes.

"When *Fear and Trembling* came out, we knew we were in trouble," Damadian said. "That meant that he was really depressed. Then he would get everyone else stirred up and he wouldn't do any work. He was very persuasive. When he turned negative, everyone else in the lab turned negative."

Goldsmith was tormented by the question of what the point of existence was. As he puts it, "What is the purpose of being? What are you trying to do?" A few times he engaged Damadian in discussions about such questions—he even gave him a book he thought might interest him, *The Tibetan Book of the Dead*—but Damadian was not particularly smitten by philosophy, nor was anyone else in the lab. Goldsmith would find consolation in Kierkegaard. "I can summarize his conclusion as being that a rational being in an irrational universe is just an absurdity and there is no real purpose to existence and the only way to see any purpose is to accept another absurdity, which is faith, to have absolute faith in God. What I got out of *Fear and Trembling* was just that. Kierkegaard answered absurdity with another absurdity—absolute irrational faith. I followed that in my way."

After a time, Goldsmith came to an answer to what the purpose of being was. "Basically, I came to Aristotle's answer, which is that man has to think to be satisfied. That is his biologically driven necessity." But the answer didn't stay with him. "Eventually I would conclude that it's an irrational question. I'm probably at least fifteen IQ points short of answering that question."

Every day seemed to bring new problems and new pressures—a part that absolutely wouldn't fit, word that another lab was making unmistakable progress. The sheeted eyes of the team members told any visitor all he cared to know. As the mental load on the group increased, the fights between Goldsmith and Minkoff continued off and on. Some days, the acrimony would bring the whole lab to a standstill. "To hear some of the epithets they hurled at each other," Damadian said, "you'd swear they had never spent a friendly millisecond together." Joel Stutman, for one, several times feared that they would come to blows. One afternoon, the two of them went at it with particular venom. Damadian finally shouted, "You two are being childish. You're acting like children."

Minkoff was phenomenal around machines. He could fix a piece of equipment that he had never laid eyes on before. And the speed at which he could do it was astonishing. This provoked envy and was nettling to Goldsmith and others in the lab. On the other hand, if you attempted to talk to Minkoff about conceptual matters, about theoretical approaches, he was at a loss. That was where Goldsmith shone. These contrary abilities fueled the dissension between the two.

There were other differences. Goldsmith was loquacious and deft with words. Communication skills, however, were not Minkoff's forte. When Goldsmith began to spew his vilification over Minkoff, Minkoff would get tongue-tied. To escape the lash of Goldsmith's tongue, he simply exploded in rage. Goldsmith used to refer snidely to Minkoff as "aphasic." The word is a medical term often used in reference to a person stricken by a stroke; he wants to say something but it comes out a garbled grunt. The one obvious weakness of Goldsmith that Minkoff exploited when pressed too hard was Goldsmith's enormous girth. He would pound away at that.

Some members of the lab team felt that Damadian more often than not favored Minkoff during the wars, though his basic approach to the ongoing combat continued to be to stroke both egos without seeming to take sides. As Jason

Koutcher has said: "Damadian switched sides between the two of them in order to get the most out of both of them. I would say Damadian tried to walk a tightrope."

The combustion did have certain beneficial aspects as the tension in the lab built. As Koutcher would remember: "I'll say one good thing about the rivalry between Minkoff and Goldsmith. It provided some comic relief, and we needed it."

Egged on by Damadian, driven less by hope than by exasperation, Goldsmith ate up several more tense weeks scouring for shorts in the magnets. He used an ohmmeter, running it up and down and all across the hoops. Had the shorts been in the middle of the magnets, that would have been an irreparable situation. The magnets would simply have had to be junked. Fortunately, they turned up on the special switch plate that Goldsmith had designed. Insulation was wound around each of the hoops and the magnets were done.

The dewars were nowhere near done. The difficulties involved in their construction were far greater than Damadian had anticipated. Both magnets sat for weeks and then months. As time passed, Goldsmith's blood pressure climbed; smoke always seemed ready to issue from his ears. Here he had wanted to build another small prototype before he embarked on the human magnet, but Damadian had nixed the idea because of time. Now he was done and the dewars were holding up everything else. Goldsmith found yet another reason to be embittered toward Minkoff. As far as Goldsmith was concerned, the pressure had been misapplied. Minkoff was the one who deserved it.

"Larry was under a lot of pressure," Stutman said. "He showed a lot of tension—mainly over the dewar. He must have worried a lot about the dewar springing a pinhole leak. He couldn't afford a pinhole leak. He was ready to fly off the handle at the slightest provocation. All you had to do was look at him cross-eyed. He would yell at anybody, though mostly Mike."

The effect of all the tension was a heightening of Damadian's nervousness. Time was precious. Never far from Damadian's mind was the prospect that one of the other labs would beat him. He fretted. He worked still longer hours. His eyes were often rimmed in red. The worst fear of all, of course, was that Paul Lauterbur would win out.

By all appearances, Lauterbur seemed to have the lead. In the summer of 1976, a symposium of medical researchers called the Gordon Conference was held in Tilton, New Hampshire. Its subject was biological applications of NMR. Lauterbur and some members of his laboratory showed up at the event with images of a rat showing a tumor growing in it and a detailed image of a green pepper that clearly delineated its interior structure. Waylan House, who had a doctorate in NMR work and was a research associate in Lauterbur's lab, attended the conference, and his recollection of the reception is: "We were hot. It was exciting. I had never seen anything before the green pepper that was really good, that was anything more than a blob. We were all hot to trot."

The other image that House particularly liked was one of tubes of water placed in the shape of an H (for House) that he had done around the same time. He subsequently gave the picture to his parents. House was responsible for much of the technical work that was done in the Stony Brook lab. "I was kind of the executor" is how he likes to put it. Despite the attention being heaped on Lauterbur, according to House, he was still fairly far from achieving a human image. "Lauterbur was hardly ever there. Typically he was gone a week and a half every month."

As House remembered it, Lauterbur did not perceive Damadian as being much of a worry. "He didn't think Damadian was capable of producing an image. He thought he was some crazy doctor at Downstate."

"Yeah," House went on, "the story at the time was that Damadian was a wacky doctor at Downstate. Phonymar is what his technique was called at Stony Brook."

House joined Lauterbur's lab at the beginning of 1974. He first lived in a rooming house before finding a cheap rental in a nearby town, and he did almost nothing but work. "If you ever go to the lab, there's a spot on the floor just to the left front of the magnet I worked on where the pattern is worn off the linoleum. That's where I stood for months on end making mechanical adjustments on that magnet." House ate all his meals out, and all at the same place, a Pancake House. He drank coffee by the gallon, and he was forever being chided by his colleagues for leaving his cup behind. Years later, when he quit the lab after his relationship with Lauterbur deteriorated, he was presented with a coffee cup with a chain on it.

When asked what Lauterbur was like, House answered, "Lauterbur was the kind of guy given to lots of strokes of genius—about one out of ten would work. There are some scientists who believe that the idea is everything. One lightbulb, one magic moment of revelation, is what it's all about. There are other scientists who believe that ideas are a dime a dozen. They think that execution is what's important. Paul was the former kind. If you think that you're Zeus and when your head splits the world changes and that's all you have to do— sit rocking in your chair and throw things at the wall—then nothing will happen."

He added, "He certainly had an ego problem. I wasn't married and was very much a workaholic. I felt responsible for everything, because no one else seemed able to do anything. I was the one who knew the art. So I typically worked eighty-hour weeks. Lauterbur worked long hours when he was there, too. One night I asked him why he worked so hard. He had a wife, some kids. And he said, 'Well, I guess one does it for the approbation of one's peers.' I walked down the hall with my coffee cup and went into my office and closed the door and laughed my head off. I sure wasn't going to work eighty hours a week for the approbation of my peers. The hell with them. But he was a man who cared about reputation. He wanted accolades."

Still, the mere mention of Lauterbur's name was enough to get an explosive rise out of Damadian. Don Vickers, who after the demise of NMR Specialties had founded his own NMR equipment company called Seimco, came to Downstate one day to deliver a spectrometer that Damadian planned to use with the human scanner to send and receive the radio waves. Damadian, who feared that Vickers would report to Lauterbur that he was in the midst of building a human scanner, draped curtains all around the areas where the pieces of the device were kept. Seeing the curtains, Vickers's curiosity was piqued and he tried everything he could think of to get a look at what was behind them. During his inquisitive loitering, Damadian trailed him like a shadow. "Looking for something?" Damadian said. "Oh, no," Vickers replied. "Just stretching my legs." After hooking up the spectrometer and receiving Damadian's grunt of thanks, Vickers told Damadian, "Now either you pay for this in thirty days or I'm going to install a secret transmitter that will send all of your data to Lauterbur." Damadian didn't laugh.

As the lights burned longer and longer at the Downstate lab, the demands of the machine began to have personal consequences. Damadian's world became circumscribed by his duplex laboratory. Home was rarely more than a place to sleep, and sometimes not even that. Any number of days, he worked right through the night, taking no rest breaks at all, and didn't return home until the following day. His wife learned enormous patience. "I guess I got used to it," she once said. "I often wondered if I should have been more demanding or if it was my gift to him to give him his freedom and let him do what he wanted. I would think that he'll suffer some day family-wise, because nobody will know him. I pictured him taking some time off to finally spend with his family and they'd all be gone and he'd feel bad. I don't know that we've ever been a normal family—when the father comes home at five o'clock and there are weekends and vacations together. We had vacations together, but that was about it. He would rarely be home for dinner on weeknights. He'd say, 'I'll be home at five,' and then midnight would come. He always had an excuse that made it seem important."

Even though he held a regular position at Hunter College, Stutman found himself spending the better part of his ever-lengthening working day at Downstate, and the load began to unravel his marriage. "I was easily there eight to ten hours a day—nights, weekends. Weekends, I was there maybe thirty hours. I'd come in from Hunter at maybe four in the afternoon and I'd have a schedule of things to accomplish. If I was lucky and nobody talked to me, I'd get that schedule done by midnight and I'd go home. Often, Larry or Mike would come in and talk, or Raymond would come in, and I wouldn't get home until two or three."

Stutman's wife was several shades less understanding of her husband's moonlighting than was Damadian's. "All of our wives were angry about us spending so much time at the lab," he said. "They reacted in different ways. My wife finally decided that I was just more interested in working on this thing than I was in her, and so my marriage broke up. This kind of work environment obviously wasn't very conducive to relating well to your wife. But I couldn't get away from the work. I felt that with a little extra effort we could bring this project off. I thought there was going to be a payoff in the end. A pot of gold. I didn't know what it would be. It's playing pinball. You work hard to get interesting work in order to get more interesting work. It's what makes scientists and engineers work. I wasn't looking all that much for money. I was looking for interesting work. And I believed in the dream. I believed in Damadian's dream."

ELEVEN

Damadian and Minkoff, as usual, were working late. "I really wonder," Damadian said without preamble, "will these dewars ever, ever get done?"

Minkoff said nothing. What was there to say? At this point, his guess was no better than anyone else's.

Arms propped up on his knees, his head in his hands, Damadian sat stoically in the laboratory, eyeing the floor vacantly. Minkoff sat slump-shouldered near him. Their hair was unruly. Their complexions were pale. Their conversation was freighted with more subdued vocabulary than was the custom. Metal parts lay strewn all over the floor, and their enthusiasm was as scattered as the parts. They were beginning to feel imprisoned by the machine.

A baffling problem had developed with one of the vacuum cans, the outermost doughnut of the dewar. Damadian said, "We decided the magnet had to be able to come apart in the event we did something wrong, which was always a safe bet. You don't know if you've built the magnet right until it's all done and stuck in the liquid helium. So we made the dewar so it could come apart. But it couldn't leak. We figured we could acccomplish this with an O-ring. In the outer can we had a groove that would take the O-ring. However, we warped it a little bit during the welding and when we put it together it leaked like a sieve. It didn't look like we'd get it sealed. We rewelded some of it, bent it, and twisted it. We tested for leaks by trying to pump it down. If you can't pump down, you have leaks. We couldn't pump it down. So we had leaks, but they weren't obvious. We went around and sprayed soapy water on the seal and if it bubbled that meant a bad leak. In the end, we had to have a seal that wouldn't let in even a few molecules.

"Well, we had dozens of leaks all over the place. A leak didn't have to be much. A molecular hole would let the gas in. When a leak was found, we'd pass a welding torch over it to seal it. Even after we checked the seal, we still found leaks in the aluminum itself—it was leaking right through the pores. So we had to weld those shut. We had to comb over the whole body of that structure. We were the Dutch boys with our fingers in the dike."

All of the welding was executed by the nimble Minkoff, who had acquired the greater part of his welding tutelage from a three-part series on the subject that *Popular Science* magazine coincidentally and thankfully published while he was at work on the dewars. Even though he began to master the principles, he ran into a weedy tangle of difficulties because the industrial welding rod he was using contained too much thermal conductivity. As a result, when the dewar was cooled down, the joints cooled too quickly and cracked. Minkoff had to reweld them. "I burned myself a lot," he said, rather ruefully. "One night I must have burned myself a dozen times. It was one of those real Pavlovian experiences. You learn not to do certain things because they hurt too much."

The dewar work was not conducive to haste. Almost a year went by before Minkoff and Damadian finally succeeded in getting one complete nest of doughnuts finished. Then they had to stand it up, a back-aching task in itself. It had been assembled lying down, and it weighed roughly a thousand pounds. Damadian went to a hardware store and purchased a block and tackle ("lousy stuff, made in Taiwan, it was always breaking"), then a pipe was attached to the ceiling as an anchor for the tackle. All the muscle in the lab, which usually meant about eight people, then hoisted it up. (Heavy objects were continually being moved about the room, and whoever happened to be handy would be recruited to help. An engineer who did some consulting work for Damadian used to say that he truly enjoyed visiting the lab because he always got a good workout. He'd leave the lab sweating bullets.)

Next, Damadian and Minkoff had to build a reservoir tank to store extra liquid helium, which would be attached to the dewar with a big elbow. The magnet would have to be replenished daily, at dementing expense, like a heavy drinker on a binge. But the storage chamber leaked intolerably. Methodically, they went over it with a special device called a Veeco model MS17-AM helium leak detector. As the device was passed up and down the tank, it picked up about as many holes as might be found in a sponge. "It took weeks and weeks to find and fix the leaks," Damadian said. "That was much of the building process. We had leaks that nobody could figure out. I worked out elaborate detective schemes to try to find them."

The leak-detection work took the team to new depths of frustration. "There were some wild moments at three or four in the morning when we were welding that storage can," Damadian remembered. "Larry and I would be welding it and we'd spot a leak. We'd put the leak detector on it and find a seam leaked. We'd mark it and Larry would get out his welding torch and his visor and weld it. We'd set up the leak detector again, which was an involved process. And sure enough, the leak wasn't there anymore. Guess what? It had moved an inch. Back out came the welding torch, Larry's visor, the asbestos gloves. And he'd weld that spot. Then we'd hook up the leak detector. And the leak would be gone. Guess what? It had moved back to where it was before. I remember once when, after that happened for hours, Larry whipped off his visor and threw it across the room. It must have sailed ten yards. He hurled his gloves in the other direction. And he threw the torch down and said, 'That's it! That is finally it!' 'No, Larry, don't give up now,' I'd tell him. 'Please don't give up now.' And I'd manage to calm him down and we'd start welding again. Oh, it was frustrating. Some days were just crushing."

Long done with his assignment, Goldsmith would lumber into the lab these days around nine or so and traipse up to the sixth floor, where he would relax and have coffee with some of the graduate students for hours. Minkoff would burn up. "My feeling," he said, "was he was taking up more air space than anything else. Quite a bit of air space, at that."

Time was no longer Damadian's friend. The whole project was taking so long, the fear of being beaten had become such a palpable presence in the lab, the problems with leaks had gotten so acute that Damadian made the decision to junk the second dewar and commit the future of the project to just one. That would mean a riskier type of magnet, no longer a Helmholtz pair and one that was not likely to have as controllable a field. But what other choice was there? As far as Damadian could see, he had no time left at all. Thus the irritable Goldsmith ended up with a hoop of wire that he never even got around to testing. At this point, though, it was not only Goldsmith who was wondering if the big machine would ever be finished.

Late one evening, Goldsmith took the elevator down to the cafeteria to grab a bite to eat before returning to several more hours of work. A prominent faculty member in the pharmacology department spied him sitting alone, munching his dinner. He left his own table and came over to where Goldsmith sat. He more or less said, "Why don't you stop what you're doing, because it's an embarrassment to the university. It's humiliating. Nothing will ever come of that nonsense that

Damadian's fiddling around with. It's utterly preposterous. Get out of there and do something with your life before it's too late. The guy is a failure."

Another time, a friend of Goldsmith's who had been a graduate student in the physiology department at Downstate wrote him a letter in which he concluded, "I urge you to get out on your own and abandon all ties to Dr. Damadian."

"This was typical of the feeling around us," Goldsmith said. "It was terribly annoying. What people were telling me basically was that I was a fool for working with Damadian."

One day, Damadian was speaking on the phone to a quite reputable scientist at MIT when the man, making a mental connection, said, "Oh, now I know who you are. You're the one who's going to build a big NMR scanner that you can put a patient into. Ho, ho, ho." After Damadian insisted that he would succeed, the scientist added, "Rots of ruck."

On yet another occasion, Damadian and his wife were invited to a fair-sized dinner party in Forest Hills. A woman arrived and was introduced to Damadian by the host. She was a doctor of internal medicine, somewhere in her fifties, who treated many cancer patients at a respected New York hospital. As he invariably did when meeting someone new, Damadian began talking animatedly about his work and the machine that he felt would help slay cancer. Growing noticeably distressed, the woman interrupted Damadian and barked, "Well, that's all fine and good. But if you accomplish all that you say, then who is going to pay the tuition for my son in college?" And she walked off in a huff, leaving Damadian stunned. He was talking about saving lives and all she cared about was losing patients and income. He dismissed her as a nut. When the party was breaking up, the woman's husband went up to Damadian and said brusquely, "My wife tells me you're a fool." And, with that, he sped out the door.

Damadian, however, never wavered in his belief. There

was a dedication of body and soul to the project that would not wane. "He was always moving," Stutman said. "He was like a boxer. He was always up. I didn't get the impression that he was depressed. I didn't get the impression that he was anxious about things. If it were me, I would have just found something else to do with my life. I mean, really! I would have gone and found something much, much easier to do, which, of course, would have been just about anything."

When Damadian was asked if he was especially sensitive to criticism, he replied immediately no, he was like anybody else, that it made him very unhappy to hear his work mocked. His attitude, he said, was "I'll show them. Rather than pack it in, I'll show them." Attempting to explain the hold the project had on him, he added, "I suppose that I thought the compensation for my unpopularity was that eventually the truth would become plain, and I'd be vindicated. Never did I think that I wouldn't be vindicated. I was so naive that I didn't know that. So I guess that allowed me to deal with the unpopularity."

Moreover, Damadian had never entirely fit in with his peers, a fact that was never lost on him. "I sang soprano growing up. When other boys my age were twice my size and beating each other up on the streets, I was singing in a high-pitched voice. When I started the Lymph Notes, it was sort of a joke until it got going. I played the violin. I was laughed at. That was considered a sissy thing to do. The same with tennis back then. The real men, naturally, played baseball and football. The sissies played tennis. What could I do? I was different. I enjoyed these things. I got laughed at for being an egghead. Good students got laughed at. Then I went to the University of Wisconsin and I was fifteen and everyone else was eighteen. I was Little Lord Fauntleroy. In medical school I was one of four Gentiles. So I was different there, too. I couldn't help it. I was always different."

More than this, he was continually haunted by a desire to spread what he felt was the truth. "I felt that if I have a piece of truth to tell, it's my duty to tell it no matter what the consequences to me. I've always felt that the truth is something you have to have the courage to say. I don't know why I feel that. I guess it's cowardly not to. I guess it's the essence of scientific integrity. If you're interested in your ability to make progress as a scientist, then it's dependent on your power to recognize the truth and act on it. If I ignore the truth of experiments, then I run a real risk of spending the rest of my life in blind alleys. So it becomes very clear that if you want to get anywhere in science you have to have faith in the truth of your experiments. You can always design enough experiments to test the truth of a result. I think where scientists have problems is sticking to the truth when it's unpopular. And if I'm going to spend ten years of my life on some experiment, I want to make sure I'm going to get something out of it. It wouldn't matter if twenty-five million people told me I was a good guy and accomplished something. That wouldn't satisfy me. I would have to see something tangible."

One way that he kept the faith was to study the history of science and remind himself of what others had gone through. "Every time I go into a new field I read biographies of the people who have been successful in the past. I realize that all these scientists had difficult times in their lives and it wasn't too different from what I was going through." A favorite story of his concerns Alexander Fleming. "Fleming discovered penicillin in the 1920s and they just ignored it and laughed at him and they wouldn't use it. When the war broke out and the English were taking large battlefield losses from the Germans and they were losing lots of people to wound infections, there was an urgent press for a cure to infection. The need yielded the scientists Florey and Chain, who resurrected Fleming's papers and together implemented and manufactured Fleming's magic solution. So he waited twenty years. Another famous story was the discovery of the cancer virus by Peyton Rouse in the 1930s. He found that by transferring leukemia in chickens, if you filtered the blood, you were unable to transmit it. That suggested it was a submicroscopic particle. And he did not get any recognition until he was eighty-nine."

When his wife, an expert on her husband's stamina, was asked about the completeness of his fixation, she replied, "He's always been incredibly tenacious. He just knew it would work and would revolutionize medicine. I think he has great faith in the Lord and that with His help he'd be able to do this and get through all these things. When there was no money, he'd spend time reading the Bible and praying. And I'd know that's what he had on his mind. And the Lord always seemed to look after him."

Other theories were formulated about what drove Damadian. Waylan House offered this explanation: "I would cast Damadian as an Othello. He needed, in my opinion, an opposite player, an opponent, and Lauterbur was clearly his opponent, as was the establishment. I feel quite sure that he would never have attempted to build that magnet if he hadn't had those opponents to stoke his engines."

Joel Stutman watched Damadian with fascination, and over the months and then years he began to construct his own hypothesis. "I often wondered how he survived. A normal human being couldn't do it. He could have simply gone out and become a physician and seen his wife a lot and played golf every Wednesday. But somewhere there was this promise to his father that he would be great. And that promise couldn't be broken. That's my feeling. Nobody gave to his children like Raymond's father gave to him. To his father, Raymond was God. Raymond had to become the Armenian Einstein. I had this conversation once with Raymond about his father, and I thought I came very close to understanding what makes Raymond run. I met him and his parents at a picnic and I had a long talk with his father. I told Raymond that his father seemed very, very sharp. I said I thought his mother reminded me of my mother—an authentic Jewish mother, the one who would really take charge in a family. He said that may be true, but he said it was his father who let him know he could do all these things. His father gave him the self-confidence. I don't know if it's self-confidence or it's guilt. I think there's a lot of guilt there. I think it's as if his father laid down his life to let Raymond do the things he's done."

Some years later, Damadian told me a story that illustrated his relationship with his father. His father was suffering from Parkinson's disease and, having taken a turn for the worse, had to be admitted to the hospital, where it seemed he had only days to live. A friend of Damadian's advised him to read ten verses from the Bible on healing. The purpose was to convince his father that his work was not yet finished on earth, and thus he would be granted more time. Damadian went to the hospital and recited the verses. His father was semi-comatose, and Damadian felt a little peculiar reading the verses to someone he doubted could even hear them. He asked his father if he wanted to accept the Lord into his heart as his personal savior. To Damadian's astonishment, he felt his father squeeze his hand. He then prayed for his father's complete healing. When he left, he was in tears. He felt sure his father would be dead before the next morning. The following day, however, his father was miraculously sitting up in bed and asking for breakfast. "Later on, my father told me that he had experienced a feeling of walking down a long hallway and it was the most wonderful feeling he had ever had—there was just complete peace and tranquillity. It was wonderful. Then somebody interrupted him and said to come back."

Of his fellow Downstate professors, few were closer to Damadian during these years than Donald Gerber, a fast-talking associate professor of medicine. Recalling his sense of the man, Gerber said, "I met him in the late 1960s, and I got to know him quite well. His lab was right around the corner from here. He used to talk to me in the hall for hours. To this day, I can't understand how he accomplished so much and still had the time to shoot the breeze. He used to talk about everything from the Copernicus theory to the philosophy of science.

"He didn't have the brainiest help. They weren't golden-haired boys from Harvard. They were smart, but he had to really train them, really drive them. And, boy, they worked hard. Plus he was acting as chief negotiator for the United University Professors, our union, and going up to Albany and trying to raise our salaries. Plus he was fighting out this thing about ion transport. He was fighting that out with the scientific community. Plus the NMR was extremely technical stuff. You don't learn equations for that in medical school. Plus he was having chamber-music concerts every morning with his family. He would wake them up at six-thirty in the morning and play chamber music or something. On top of that, he was having children. On top of that, he had a house in Forest Hills and he got in a fight over who owned the lot or something. Then he had long philosophical discussions with me about scientists from decades or centuries ago. He would present his papers and refer back to these people, and I think it got some other people's goats. You don't normally present an academic paper and refer back to Copernicus or Galileo or Newton. Then he was applying for grants. What a herculean task that was. Dealing with the morons at NIH who didn't know the first thing about what a patient looked like. They would come here and pick apart his equations. They weren't always perfectly done. I suppose it's like asking a racing driver to tell you about Galileo's first three laws of gravity. I suppose they have to do with motion, but you don't need to know them to drive a car fast.

"He's got a skin as thick as a rhinoceros. He had things in good perspective. He was dealing with a bunch of small-minded nincompoops. He had the broad picture. Damadian was like a superman among midgets. I've never seen anyone like him—cutting through the red tape all the time and accomplishing everything."

Gerber was particularly equipped to empathize with Damadian's woes. Since his arrival at Downstate, his specialty had been rheumatic arthritis. He hypothesized that the affliction springs from low blood histidine concentration. Others in the field totally ignored Gerber's hypothesis. "If it turned out to be true, everyone else would be out of business," Gerber explained. Isn't Gerber bothered by the lack of attention? "Yeah, it bothers me," he said. "But there's nothing I can do about it. But, on the other hand, it pleases me. If everyone and their uncle were working on this, I wouldn't have anything to do. Damadian can operate on two levels. He can work alone or in competition with the rest of the world. I can't compete against the world. So I can work at my own pace. I have time to talk to you. I'm protected from the awful thought that tomorrow's journal will have the answer to my problem. I go my own way. It's like walking down the street naked and not having to worry about people staring at you. But I know I'm right. I see the data. Damadian and I both have persistence, and he has terrific self-confidence. There are only a small number of people—his wife, his kids, me, Eichna—who remember how much of a struggle it was for him to get this thing done. And memory plays tricks on you. For everyone else, it's a fiction. They don't know."

True, Damadian knew nothing of giving up. But despite his oceanic confidence, as the New York winter closed in and the winds began to whip along Clarkson Avenue, that cheerless old bugaboo once again started to threaten the project. A scientist must mind his purse, for it is his master as surely as it is a banker's. Salaries had to be paid. Bills were piling up like unwanted guests. The coins in the kitty were just about gone.

TWELVE

It was a thoughtful day for Damadian. In the dim, disordered laboratory, brooding about possible sources of money, he kept working with an idea. He was encouraged by the recent election of Jimmy Carter as President. Carter was still down in Plains, Georgia. "He was making all these promises," Damadian said. "Ring him up on the telephone and he'll talk to you. I swallowed all that. I felt it was an unusual opportunity. A President-elect was living in his own house in a small town; there was a reasonable chance of getting to see him. So I thought I'd go see him."

It did not strain his imagination too much to envision Carter getting him money—$200,000 was the figure Damadian had in mind. Why shouldn't he? He struck Damadian as an honest, decent man. What honest, decent man wouldn't want to do something about cancer? Moreover, unlike most of the people Damadian had approached for money, Carter certainly ought to be able to comprehend the technology. After all, he had been trained as a nuclear engineer. The project should make sense to him. Yes, Damadian thought, if he saw Carter he might get money. "I thought he was smart enough that I could make him understand. Plus I was pretty desperate. I didn't have a better idea."

Damadian brought the subject up one evening with his father-in-law, Bo Terry, who, after chewing on the idea, replied, "Well, why don't you go see Carter?"

"Well, how do I get to see him?"

"I imagine our minister could make some connections."

David Terry was appointed to approach Diego Flores, the

minister of the Terrys' Westhampton church, and to tell him about Damadian's eagerness to see Carter. When Terry asked the minister if there was any chance of getting an audience with Carter, Flores answered that he'd be happy to call the minister of the Plains Baptist Church, a man named Bruce Edwards, and see what he could do. A few days later, he reported back that Edwards said he felt quite confident that Carter would consent to see Damadian if he visited Plains. That was encouragement enough. With a refreshed sense of confidence, Damadian flew to Plains, a speck of clay smack in the middle of redneck country.

Once he got there, he checked into a cheap motel on the outskirts of town and rented a car. Not pausing to unpack, he set off to see the Rev. Mr. Edwards. At the time, Jimmy Carter was in the midst of selecting members of his cabinet, and Edwards was wary of intruding on his time. So although Damadian heaped mounds of documents and letters on him, nothing much happened. Not disposed to sit around cooling his heels, Damadian decided to take matters into his own hands. Damadian was a good talker. There were plenty of Carters floating around Plains. One of them, he figured, was bound to get him access to the one who counted.

As he poked around Plains, his mind swam with possible approaches. Just march over to Carter's house and present himself. There was no chance of that. The place was overrun with security guards. Hang around town until Carter showed up at, perhaps, the grocery store or the barber. Everywhere he went, unfortunately, he was ringed by agents. Ingratiate himself with a Carter relative who could open some doors. Maybe so.

The first couple of days, Damadian wandered aimlessly through the streets of Plains. He socialized with some of the news-hunting newspaper and TV reporters and told them about his plight, wondering if they knew of a way he might get to see Carter. They all said it was hopeless. At night, most people in Plains, including the whole of the press corps, would dine at an impromptu steak house that had been set up in a quonset hut by an enterprising local woman. Damadian would eat there, too, chatting with everyone he ran into, hoping to find a link.

One morning Damadian dropped into the antique and souvenir store on Main Street, since its proprietor happened to be a peppy man with a tomcat face named Hugh Carter, Jimmy Carter's cousin. In Hugh Carter, Damadian found an immediate ally. "A super guy," Damadian would say of him. "I hit it off with him right away. He was one of the nicest people I've ever met."

As a kid, Hugh Carter loved to fish. He used to dig up his own worms. Since experience came to teach him the prime places to find them, other kids in search of bait would come to him. Entrepreneurial wheels turned in his head. He started growing worms and selling them. When asked why he got into the worm business, he replied, "I got into it to make money." By now, he presided over an immense worm farm— the biggest, as far as he knew, in the world—and was selling the creatures by the millions. His advertisements could regularly be spotted in the back of *Popular Science* and *Field & Stream*. Hugh Carter often fell into a ruminative mood. When he found out that Damadian was a scientist, he insisted on dragging him out to the worm farm to see if he had any useful suggestions on how to improve his cultivation methods. Damadian needed money badly. If a journey to a worm farm would help, he'd go take a look at the worms.

It was a curious domain, all right. There was a nice house, and then behind the house was a big lake surrounded by beds of worms. Ushered around the farm, he gazed over the acres of wiggly creatures, baffled. "I really didn't know anything about worms. As far as I could see he was doing just fine. Those worms were growing like crazy."

Having by then heard Damadian's tale of woe, Hugh Carter was both fascinated and sympathetic. He found it exasperating that Damadian was unable to raise money to support what clearly seemed to be a worthy project. He was keen to help. He gave Damadian his business card with a note scribbled on the back: "Go to church on Sunday. Jimmy will be teaching Sunday school."

School began at nine. Taking no chances, Damadian showed up at eight. He was the first one there. As others began to gather, a church official instructed them to line up in rows of two. "There were lots of guys there talking into their lapels," Damadian said. "Presumably Secret Service men. To my surprise, though, everyone was let in and no one was searched. I thought that was pathetic security. I complained about that to one of the men, and then they all started talking into their lapels and pointing at me like I was a suspect or something."

Damadian sat in the first row. Jimmy Carter arrived and settled into the second row, beside Hugh Carter and directly behind Damadian. The night before, Hugh Carter had delivered a lengthy letter to his cousin that Damadian had written, spelling out some of the details of his research and explaining his dire need for money. When Jimmy Carter sat down, Hugh Carter pointed out Damadian and told his cousin that he was a great scientist and that he had more sense than the two of them put together. Jimmy Carter nodded and replied that he hadn't yet read the letter but that Rosalynn had and that he intended to look it over as soon as he found a free moment. Then he rose to teach Sunday school. Afterward, like the others, Damadian got to shake the President-elect's hand. That was the last he saw of him.

Hour after hour, Damadian combed the streets of Plains, like a beggar in search of a handout. Days later, still making no progress with the Carters, Damadian decided to visit Billy Carter. That was easy enough. Billy had that famous gas station, where, at the end of the day, country folk would arrive in their pickups and go into Billy's station to party. What it really was, of course, was a beer joint. The place was lined from one end to the other with a refrigerator chest crammed with beer. In shirt and tie, Damadian had perhaps not chosen the best attire in which to approach Billy Carter. He was clearly out of his element and felt the need for some hasty tutelage. "I spoke to one of the guys outside and I asked him how you got Billy's attention. He said, you say, 'Billy I want to talk to you.' Just like that. 'Billy I want to talk to you.' So I went in there and I said, 'Billy I want to talk to you.' He looked at me and I explained that I was a scientist with a valuable discovery in cancer and I needed help. And he said, 'Well, I can't talk to you right now about that.' And so I said, 'Well, when can I talk to you about this?' And he said, 'Never.' And that was the end of that."

His resolve still not shriveled, Damadian next called on a woman who was the Georgia campaign manager for Carter and told her he wanted to meet Miss Lillian, Carter's mother. That would be no problem, she said, Miss Lillian was down at the train station greeting people. "Sure enough, she sat there in a rocking chair, welcoming tourists lined up to see her, as if she was something in a museum. I thought that was a poor time to see her, so I had the woman arrange a private session. She did, and I brought in a videotape I had done with NBC and showed it to her. She took it all in and then mused out loud, 'Wouldn't it be wonderful if Jimmy cured cancer during his administration?' She never did another thing."

Hugh Carter tried his best to keep Damadian's feeble hopes alive. He assured him that if he could just be patient, things would get done once Jimmy was in the White House. He'd be invited down then and he'd receive his money. It was getting close to Christmas now, and Jimmy Carter had left Plains. Discouraged because he had failed to talk directly to the new President, Damadian flew back to Brooklyn and his Downstate lab, several hundred dollars poorer. "I was pleased that I made the contact with Hugh Carter. But I was depressed that I didn't get an audience with Jimmy. I had to get money. And I had no idea where I'd get it."

By now, matters were desperate. Running out of even far-fetched options, Damadian was seriously thinking about laying off members of his team. The thought was acutely painful, but the money wasn't there for their salaries or for the liquid helium to feed the magnet. For so long, Damadian had felt like Moses standing on the mountain showing the others in the lab the promised land, but now even he felt beaten down. Months had been spent building a human scanner, and Damadian began to wonder if his dream was destined simply to gutter out.

Several weeks later, deliverance came. Damadian chanced to meet a man from Nashville named Bill Akers. He knew nothing of what Damadian was doing, and not even lengthy explanations and blackboard scribblings really helped him understand. When Damadian met with him and explained his needs, he seemed interested but not overly enthusiastic. Damadian had no notion that the man would present him with even a dollar. Bill Akers, however, was to become Damadian's savior.

The identification on the door of Akers's Nashville office is "The Parent Company." The company doesn't actually do much of anything, according to Akers, but is simply a place for him and his brother, J. Clarke Akers III, "to hang our hats." The Akerses are civil engineers and once owned an asphalt business in Nashville. Several years ago, they sold it to a Tennessee company and retired at an age when retirement could be fun. Bill spends a good part of his time hunting quail. His brother hunts deer.

Bill Akers is a well-built man with thin white hair and a guileless manner that makes him seem younger than he is. With a broad smile, he ushered me into his office, dropped into a seat behind a desk, and swiveled back and told me how he came to be Damadian's saving angel.

"I was raising money for Vanderbilt Engineering School—I was an alumnus—so I asked Don Elliott, a friend and a consultant, to help me. I was traveling a lot with him and so forth, seeing him quite a bit more than I normally would, and he told me that he had a girl working for him—Judith Watson—and he said her husband, Jack Watson, was a first-class scientist in mass spectography, whatever the hell that is. He's such a scientist that this spectograph was named after him and another guy. So Elliott told me that another scientist was on to something really important and Watson would stake his reputation not only on what he was doing but on the fact that he would do something significant. But he needed help. So I said, 'Why, what are we waiting for? Let's go see him.' So we did. We hunted him out in Downstate in all those catacombs and we talked to the man."

Akers, of course, had no background that was of even minuscule help in judging the merits of Damadian's research. Standing there in the messy Downstate labs, his eyes glazing over as the words poured out of Damadian's mouth, he made up his mind purely on his sense of the man.

"I was very much impressed with the guy's sincerity and knowledge, and he was an ordinary kind of guy. Except, of course, he was a genius. But he wasn't some sort of off-the-wall nutty kind of guy—and there are lots of them. He was obsessed. There was no doubt about that. But he was a normal kind of guy. A nice wife. Normal kids that give you all the kinds of problems that kids give you. And he had a vision. He wanted to cure cancer."

Here and there, Akers had been approached before by people who felt they had a vision that needed nothing more than a bit of money for it to come true. A person once presented him with an idea for a paving machine. Just too impractical, was Akers's judgment. Someone else came along with a technique for waterproofing. "He was just too way out. He thought you could use it for everything and solve all the world's problems. There's not a roof that doesn't leak. But we couldn't keep him hitched to one thing. He wanted to use it for toothpaste, is how my brother put it." Damadian, though, struck him as a man with his mind fastened to one idea, and an idea that was about as important as ideas could get. Akers, though he had no familiarity with cancer, knew it was never far away.

After visiting with Damadian for two hours, Akers made up his mind that he was going to try to help the man out. For the better part of a year, Akers and Elliott, while attempting to attract money for Vanderbilt, did some moonlighting to round up funding for Damadian. Akers had a friend who worked for Laurance Rockefeller. He helped Akers get to see one of Rockefeller's chief aides. He wrote to Daniel Ludwig, the billionaire shipbuilder generally assumed to be one of the half-dozen richest men in the United States. "I just tried everything," Akers told me. "They all listened and were very attentive, but nobody signed a check."

In March 1977, Akers happened to fly to New York to attend a wedding. By this time, he had become better acquainted with Damadian, and he and his wife, JoAnn, took Damadian and Donna out to dinner. Afterward, Damadian drove the Akerses back to the hotel where they were staying, and before saying goodbye they sat for a moment in the car. "I asked him how he was doing," Akers recalled. "He said, 'Bill,

I'm running out of money and I'm about to lose my team.' He said, 'If I don't get money by April 1, I'm going to have to fold it up.' I said, 'Raymond, how much do you need—a million dollars, a hundred thousand dollars? What is it that you need?' And he gave me a figure—ten thousand dollars. So I said, 'I'm going to go home and try to raise it.' And I said, 'If I can't, I'm going to give it to you.' And I came back and tried to raise it and couldn't and so I gave him a personal check." Akers then paid a visit to his brother and to two friends, James Stewart and John Rich. "And I told them that I had given this cat ten thousand dollars, why don't you give him ten thousand dollars, too. And they did, because I asked them to. They had plenty of money."

Jim Stewart had been in the steel business; he had sold his company and was flush. John Rich was in coal; giving away money was not a strain for him, either. Not that his friends were at all confident that the checks they had signed were money well spent. In fact, when Akers stopped by to pick up the ten thousand dollars from Rich, Rich's wife greeted him with a half-smile and said, "John left the crazy money for you."

No strings were attached to the $40,000 that flowed from Nashville to Brooklyn. Speaking of the gift, Akers said, "When I gave Raymond the ten thousand dollars, I told him I didn't want anything except two things. I wanted to be invited to Stockholm when he got the Nobel Prize and I didn't want to have to wait in any line if I ever had to get in that machine."

Damadian had to pinch himself to make sure he wasn't dreaming; his confidence soared like a kite that had caught a sharp gust of wind. "I felt terrific. I didn't need to drive home that night. I could have floated all the way. I was going to finish my project. I felt nothing could stop me now. It would take masked men with guns to stop us now."

With the new infusion of funds, work percolated again. More liquid helium was purchased. Salaries were paid. The dewar was finished. It was quite possibly the biggest dewar ever made. It had taken most of the year to build it and rid it of leaks. Or, at least, rid it of as many leaks as the team could possibly manage. As it was, the thing still was imperfect enough that fresh supplies of liquid helium had to be transferred daily into the dewar from the storage container. Hu and Goldsmith most often found themselves saddled with transfer duty. The leaking helium that vanished into the air was costing Damadian something like $2,000 a week.

Minkoff built a seat for a subject to sit on while being scanned. Calling it a seat is perhaps inaccurate. It was really nothing more than a skinny wooden rail about six inches wide and about twenty feet long, and it was designed so that it could move backward and forward as well as sideways, thus allowing different parts of the body to be investigated. Initially Damadian thought he would keep the patient stationary and move the magnet across his body, but it now seemed more practical to move the patient. The seat was affixed to two platforms that sat on scissor mounts. There were no motors on the platforms to move the rail automatically; when it was time to do a scan, someone would have to shove the subject around.

Before the machine would be complete, a probe or coil to wrap around the subject of the scan to allow the radio waves to be fired into him was still necessary. The coil, in essence an antenna, would be attached to a coaxial cable attached in turn to a radio transmitter, which would pick up the signals emitted by the body. It was thought to be a fairly routine chore. Probes had been built in the lab before by Damadian and Goldsmith for the smaller NMR machines, and there never had been any particular difficulties. NMR Specialties had provided a set of equations that determined the proper capacitors to use to make coils of various sizes. A coil contained three or four capacitors that had to be of the proper values to match the impedance of the receiver. Without the correct capacitors, there would be no signal. The responsibility for the antenna fell to Goldsmith. Using the equations, he and Damadian designed a solenoid coil that was four feet in diameter, and they had the carpentry shop build it.

When it was attached to the magnet and a phantom (tubes of water arranged in a pattern) was placed inside to emit a signal, it fizzled. There was no signal at all. No one could understand it. It simply didn't work. "We calculated that it would work and it didn't," Goldsmith said.

Was it the coil? Or was it the magnet? Damadian inserted a small test coil, less than an inch in diameter, that he knew worked. A signal was received from the phantom. The magnet, therefore, worked. The problem was the antenna.

Damadian instructed Goldsmith to build coils of increasingly larger sizes to see how they would perform. A two-inch antenna picked up a signal. So did a three-inch antenna, though the signal was worse. A four-inch coil still produced a signal, but it was even worse. When a five-inch antenna was tried, there was no signal at all. It became apparent to Damadian and Goldsmith that NMR Specialties' equations for determining the capacitors were faulty. The plain fact was that though they were accurate enough to produce workable antennas of small size, they were useless for antennas of more than a few inches. Neither Damadian nor Goldsmith felt confident that they could devise new equations. And so Damadian told Goldsmith to simply start building antennas by trial and error and see how large he could go.

"I had some serious doubts about whether this was ever going to work," Goldsmith said. "After all, nobody had done this. We never dreamed that there would be a problem. This was a surprise problem. It dawned on us that we wouldn't be able to build a coil that was large enough to be of any use. If we couldn't, the rest of the machine would be useless. The whole project would be a bust."

When Goldsmith expressed his doubts to Damadian, Damadian looked at him and said sharply, "Just keep doing it."

The words had their intended effect, though Goldsmith was agitated. "I resented that," Goldsmith said testily. "It's easy to say to go back there and do it some more, to go back there and screw around some more. Trial and error is a very frustrating way of doing anything. I went back and did it some more, but more and more resentfully."

For weeks and then months, Goldsmith built antennas, testing them with different pairs of capacitors until he got them working and then advancing in size. Meanwhile, to get the original four-foot coil out of the way, Goldsmith strung it up by wire from the ceiling, where it hung, as he liked to put it, "like the whale in the Museum of Natural History."

Goldsmith had no idea why some capacitors worked and others didn't. He was just reaching out in the dark. "I was working on pure intuition at this point. I'd roll over a cart with a whole collection of capacitors—maybe a few hundred—and we'd have our phantom in the latest coil and there wouldn't be a signal. So I'd pull a capacitor out of the drawer and I'd say, 'Hmmm, this feels like the right value,' and I'd go and solder it onto the coil and everyone would laugh. I was going on nothing other than intuition."

Goldsmith fabricated dozens of coils, looking for the optimum size. To make his antennas, he used plastic or tough cardboard that was then wrapped with copper wire. Where did he get the cardboard? He slashed apart the big garbage bins in the lab. While he worked, he fought the fear that no coil big enough to contain a human could be built.

Meanwhile, Minkoff and Damadian toyed with a different idea. Whichever coil worked first would be used. Goldsmith's antenna was designed for a patient who would be sitting down; Minkoff was experimenting with one that would encircle a supine patient. It was a saddle coil. He took two loops of wire and put one to each side of a cylinder so that they didn't actually touch each other. Before Goldsmith was done, Minkoff managed to get a signal from his antenna. However, he couldn't get the signal to focus. There was no spatial localization. Minkoff couldn't explain what was happening, and Goldsmith, who didn't understand it either, dubbed the strange phenomenon the "Minkoff effect."

Goldsmith managed to construct a nine-inch coil that produced a signal. It was still clearly too small to contain a body, but it could easily have handled a head or an arm. Goldsmith urged Damadian to try to get an image of a head.

"No," Damadian said stiffly, "we're going for the body."

"He wanted to go straight for the human image," Goldsmith said. "That was first down for him. I thought we should pick up some yards while we could. But he wanted to go for a first down."

The fiftieth coil Goldsmith built was fourteen inches in diameter, barely large enough to encircle a human chest. It worked. Goldsmith tried sixteen inches without much success and so decided that fourteen was the upper limit. Neither he nor Damadian understood why fourteen inches worked and sixteen didn't, but answering that question was not a priority. Fourteen inches would have to do. The antenna was made out of garbage-bin cardboard and copper foil tape. It was the last piece of the scanner to be completed.

So they were done. It was June 1977. A sense of exhilaration rippled over the weary crew. Damadian felt the relief of a reprieved felon.

"I could hardly believe it was done," he said. "I thought it would never be finished. There was a great sense of relief. There was still no sense that it was all worth it. We didn't yet know if it would work with someone in it. It was still an all-or-nothing situation. Either it was going to work and rockets were going to go off or nothing was going to happen and we would be the laughingstocks of the scientific community."

In the event that the silver machine did go down in history, Damadian wanted it to have a suitably evocative name. Over the long months, Minkoff had applied assorted undignified names to it. He also liked to call it "that sign for Dunkin' Donuts." He would tease the team that if they never got it to work, why, they could always sell it to Dunkin' Donuts. Early in the project, Damadian had told the others that they would paint the finished machine red, white, and blue, in honor of the American Bicentennial. But with all the delays, the Bicentennial had come and gone. Damadian stared hard at the machine, thought of the spirit that had gone into it, and christened it Indomitable.

Before them stood a mammoth metal device that had a beauty about it in the eyes of its creators but was undeniably ugly and crude to any outsider. It looked like the science project of a kid who had gotten more than a little carried away. It was a big circular thing that vaguely resembled the slowly turning wheel in a fun house that you try to walk through without losing your balance. A storage chamber sat at the very top of the wheel, resembling an industrial coffee maker laid on its side. A narrow wooden plank pierced the center of the wheel, like some sort of balance beam. The cardboard coil was attached to it. The whole thing looked like a medieval torture chamber. The exact nature of the torture was not immediately clear but there was no doubt that it would not be fun inside there. It seemed like something to stay away from. The question that hung over the lab now was which one of them would sit inside of it when the juice was turned on.

167

THIRTEEN

Some eight possibilities existed, when one counted up the graduate students and technicians regularly working with Damadian. The lab was innocent of volunteers. Anyone who sat inside the scanner would be surrounded by a magnet with a field strength of perhaps five thousand gauss. There were going to be radio pulses bombarding his body. No adverse effects had been detected in animals that had undergone the test, but no person had ever been inside the machine. While they worked around the magnet, Damadian and a few members of the team had experienced headaches that caused some grogginess and confusion. Jotting down notes, Damadian would find himself misspelling words, and the machinists complained that they were making errors because of the headaches. Damadian worried about that. Feet shuffled, eyes rolled from ceiling to floor, without stops in-between. Everyone was a little afraid. Some were mightily scared. "Okay," Damadian finally said. "I guess I'm your guinea pig."

"I was afraid," he later confessed. "It had never been done before. We had tested it on rats, and nobody dropped dead. But we didn't know. I felt it was my duty to go in there. Not that anyone else volunteered. But I thought it was dangerous and so it should be me because it was my pipe dream. But I was nervous, all right, that I was going to drop dead in the magnet. I was worried for weeks about the safety of it."

University red tape required scientists who might be risking their lives to secure permission from the school's human experimentation committee. No fan of tape of any color, Damadian ignored protocol. "I didn't see where they had any right to tell me whether I could stick myself in my own machine. That wasn't an option that I thought they should have. I could see them deliberating for eight months about whether to allow me to do this. Afterward, they screamed and yelled. It was too late, of course."

He didn't even bother telling Alfred Bollet, his department chairman, of his intention. (Ludwig Eichna, the previous chairman, had retired some years before.) "The department chairman couldn't have cared less what I was doing," Damadian has said. "He wouldn't have cared if I jumped out the window. Other people were looking at red blood cells and how the muscle relaxes—traditional subjects. With me, it was something out of science fiction. You'd go up to the lab and there'd be gases bubbling up and liquid nitrogen, and we were building this giant magnet. I was the university oddball. I was a genuine nuisance. I was a madman."

Before actually putting himself into Indomitable, Damadian decided to do some tests of the signal strength and resolution of the scanner. When the magnet was first turned on, its field began to drift at around one thousand gauss. Some of the wire had to be bypassed in the special access sleeve that Goldsmith had made, and as the wire went the strength of the field was sapped until it was reduced to five hundred gauss, one-tenth the level that Damadian had originally aimed for. Whether that would be enough to produce a human image was anyone's guess.

Some scanning was done of phantoms, tubs of doped water (water with nickel chloride in it to allow quick collection of the NMR signal) with some hollow tubes in them intended to simulate lungs. Damadian, Goldsmith, and Minkoff had constructed an entire family of phantoms, which they gave odd names to. The first one was called Oscar. There was also Oscar Jr., which was about nine inches across. A successful scan of Oscar Jr. was done on May 10 to check on the resolution.

Other phantoms that were successfully scanned included Harvey and Geraldine. There were also Oscarella and Oscaretta.

At about this time, several scientists from the National Institutes of Health visited Downstate to review Damadian's progress in response to another grant application he had submitted. Gathered in the conference room of the university president, they listened as Damadian explained how he had succeeded in focusing the NMR signal in a phantom. Hearing this, one of the visiting scientists, a physicist who had long worked in NMR, piped up, "Focusing a magnetic field in that way is theoretically impossible."

Well, Damadian replied, follow me. Whereupon he led the group upstairs to his laboratory. He put Goldsmith's antenna inside Indomitable, and then placed a small bottle in the center of the antenna where the focus was. The radio transmitter was turned on, and an NMR signal was picked up. The bottle was moved to a new position, and the signal vanished.

"See?" Damadian said. "It's focused."

To which one of the scientists snorted, with peculiar indifference to what he had just seen, "That proves nothing."

The grant was denied.

Doped water was ideal for testing signal strength, since there was little to interfere with a signal. But before Damadian would go into the machine, it was decided on the evening of May 10 to do a scan of a dead turkey, in order to see just how much of the signal would be lost using flesh rather than doped water. The turkey actually presented a somewhat ideal situation as well, since it was dead and didn't move. Movement significantly interfered with signal strength, too. Damadian, as was characteristic of him during many of the experiments conducted in the lab, announced that he wanted to do the turkey at the last minute. To find a specimen, he called around to several neighborhood supermarkets, but they stocked only frozen turkeys. A frozen turkey wouldn't scan. They needed a freshly killed one. But where was one to be had? It occurred to Damadian that a kosher butcher shop would necessarily have a fresh turkey on hand. He phoned one that was near Downstate. The butcher said that, sure, he had fresh turkeys, but he was quite sorry, he was just closing up for the night.

"Wait a minute," Damadian replied in his most persuasive manner. "We're not just interested in eating the thing. This is for medical research. Can't you stay open? We badly need a turkey."

The butcher, anxious to get home, pondered that argument. There was a long silence on the other end of the line. Then he said, "Well, that's all well and good for medical experiments, but why does it have to be kosher?"

After Damadian patiently explained that they needed a fresh specimen, the butcher grudgingly agreed to stay open until one of the graduate students arrived to pick up the turkey.

Once the bird was inserted in the coil and the machine turned on, it was clear that a great deal of the signal strength was lost. But the resolution seemed decent enough to achieve a human scan. The interior of the turkey could be outlined. The bird stayed in the machine for twenty-six minutes. But there was, of course, nothing historic about scanning a kosher turkey. What would be the result with a human being?

The evening of May 11, 1977, was warm and humid, the sort of night that would get one to thinking about rolling out the barbecue, and the lawn chairs. Damadian, Minkoff, Goldsmith, and several graduate students assembled in the Downstate lab. Everyone appeared a little tense. As a precaution, several doctors had been asked over from the hospital to monitor the experiment. A defibrillator and an EKG were brought along.

Like many scientists, Damadian regularly scribbled brief notes about his experiments and ideas in pale green oversized record books. On May 11, before getting into the magnet, he wrote in his notebook: "30 minutes in the field if I can stand it, 15 minutes if I can't."

Surrounded by his helpers and the doctors, haunted by fears of a bust, Damadian shrugged out of his shirt and retreated into his nerves. If this doesn't work, then what? Well, few scientific experiments succeed on the first try. It's the nature of the beast. We probably haven't got all the bugs worked out. But we ought to get at least a feeble signal. That alone will be cause for celebration. I hope we at least get a feeble signal. As these thoughts flew in and out of Damadian's mind, the doctors attached the electrocardiogram to his chest to monitor his heartbeat and alert them to any evidence of the onset of a heart attack. A blood-pressure cuff was affixed to his right arm. An EKG was wired up to his head to take a brain scan. Oxygen was kept handy. In addition to the medical gear, the cardiologist had brought a camera along, and he had some pictures taken of him attending to Damadian and posing before Indomitable. He said history was being made here tonight and he wanted evidence that he was a witness to it.

The cardboard coil was slipped over Damadian's bare chest. It was a tight fit. It seemed that if Damadian sneezed, it might burst. Damadian sat down on the hard wooden rail and realized that it was not a place you wanted to sit for long. At eight fifty-five, with a minimum of drama, the machine was turned on. Nothing.

A quick search by Goldsmith and Minkoff turned up a broken wire on the machine. Damadian was taken out of the coil while it was repaired, then put back in at seven minutes past ten. Again, the machine was turned on. Nothing.

For several hours, Goldsmith and Minkoff toyed with various possibilities. Damadian was shifted into different positions. But nothing. No NMR signal at all.

"It looked hopeless," Damadian remembers of the evening's dismal events. "It seemed to our great dismay that our armies of critics were proven right—that it was a harebrained scheme, that it was impossible!

Damadian wiggled out of the garbage-bin vest. The doctors gathered up their equipment and, after exchanging some polite pleasantries, quietly took their leave. So much for the cardiologist's snapshots of history.

The only good news was that Damadian felt fine. His blood pressure, respiratory rate, pulse rate, and electrocardiograms showed no significant changes during the exposure to the magnetic field. As he recorded in his notebook: "Virtually no adverse reaction to the time or the field. No headaches. No eye pain. Some flushing around the ears. No dizziness. Not even the usual confusion from the magnet headache."

Damadian reminded himself that few important experiments work the first time they are tried, yet his anxiety level had climbed considerably in anticipation of going into the machine, and now he was mightily depressed. "It was a depressing night, because even though you have low expectations, you have expectations. Now it was reality. Not to even get a signal. I was plenty depressed."

Whenever he plunged deep into depression, Damadian typically sought solace in sleep. "So I just went home and slept it off. It's like a bad dream. You try to have it go away. I don't know if all scientists are like this, but when something doesn't work I get depressed and I can't work. So I go to sleep. Always I'm in a much better mood in the morning. By then, I've talked myself into the fact that it's going to work. What often happens is I wake up in the middle of the night or in the morning with a solution."

No solution, however, presented itself the next morning. Still, Damadian was in a far better frame of mind. He hurried off to the lab, hopeful that someone else had thought of something. Assembled in a circle, the team tossed around ideas.

The post mortem dwelt with this or that possible mechanical shortcoming, but, in sum, they were empty of any really good ideas, other than the possibility that they still refused to believe: that the technology was a bummer. Goldsmith, in particular, felt extraordinarily frustrated. As ideas were thrown into the air and shot down like clay pigeons, Goldsmith hurled up an answer. He said, looking directly at Damadian, "Maybe you're too fat."

Damadian would subsequently recall, "You look at him and you wonder how he had the temerity to suggest it."

But yes. Perhaps. Damadian's flab was indeed spilling over the cardboard vest. The body itself conducts electricity. Too much electricity flowing from Damadian's body could very well have overloaded Indomitable's antenna and detuned it.

"The only hypothesis of any worth was that I was too big," Damadian said. "The only other alternative was that the coil couldn't be made large enough for this to work."

Discarding the possibility of slimming down Damadian, the only way to test the new hypothesis was to try a skinnier guinea pig. Eyes did not have to look far to land on the most likely subject.

Minkoff squirmed and directed his gaze at anything but the faces of the others. Well, Larry? Uh, I'm sorry, I'm not going in. But Larry! Forget it. Minkoff was all of twenty-six. He was keen on seeing twenty-seven. No ill effects showed themselves in Damadian; but, still, who knew?

Also, Minkoff still thought that his antenna idea might be the solution to Indomitable's failure. Before he would put on his rival Goldsmith's antenna and climb into the scanner, he wanted more time to try to perfect his coil. Damadian was

174

impatient. This was a race, after all. Even one day could matter. "I thought Lauterbur was much closer than I was," he said. "This thing was crashing all over the place and I thought I was never going to get there. Lauterbur didn't have to build a magnet. It just came to him in a crate. Manna from heaven."

Damadian didn't feel comfortable about ordering Minkoff into the machine. What if it wasn't safe? So he decided to bide his time and hope that his reluctant assistant would come around.

With no subject to test, Goldsmith, with supervision from Damadian, went to work on the scanner's electronics, trying to improve the all-important signal-to-noise ratio of the spectrometer. Clearly there was a lot of background noise interfering with the machine. Noise amounted to stray voltages that were picked up and disturbed performance. NMR reception is not much different from regular reception of radio signals. Getting an NMR signal from deep within the human body is analogous to trying to tune in a New York radio station out on eastern Long Island. As Goldsmith would explain, "It breaks up. You can barely hear it. You hear all sorts of background whistles and hums and bangs." With an NMR machine, background noise in any frequency can be due to a lot of things. Some noise results from thermal motion. Any of the electrosurgical devices in the hospital caused interference. Elevator motors start up and shut down, fouling things up.

"When there's too much noise," Goldsmith said, "the signal gets buried and you can't see it. The motion of a body creates some noise, too. When you have a small sample and thus a small antenna, you have a much better signal-to-noise ratio, because the sample is right next to the antenna. Also, since the antenna is so small, it's going to pick up very little extraneous noise. As you get bigger and bigger antennas, you pick up more and more noise."

The challenge facing Goldsmith was to learn, without any

past experience to guide him, to tune and impedance-match the large antenna. What was all too evident now was that the human scanner had been designed so fast, it represented such a technical leap, that it had quirks no one had ever dealt with. At this point, the tuning process was nothing like a science. It was purely an art. Conquering the challenge required imagination and a dogged persistence. Some days—days meaning twelve-hour stretches—nothing that Goldsmith tried worked. There would be long nights of sharp fears.

Goldsmith once explained the tuning process. "The antenna is a big inductor. You have to match it with the right set of capacitors to make it resonate at the right frequency of the sample. This meant choosing the right capacitors. We had some equations to calculate them, and we used these on the small coils. But they didn't work on the large coil. I didn't know why. We were dealing with approximate values. I couldn't nail it down. I would tune on the bench without the sample in it, then put the sample in and retune, and then change the capacitor level. A lot of fiddling was involved. It became apparent that Damadian detuned the antenna to such an extent that he wasn't even remotely close to the values of the capacitors that I had determined on the bench, so getting the right values was pure guesswork. And I couldn't do it. The choices were basically infinite."

Days, then weeks droned by. Goldsmith monkeyed with the coil. The work demanded that he plod. Meanwhile, Minkoff and Damadian tinkered with the Minkoff antenna. Minkoff's wife was working the night shift as a nurse, so Minkoff stayed at the lab through the night. Goldsmith worked the day shift. The lights in the lab were virtually never dark.

Though little progress was apparent with his antenna, Minkoff still would not go into Indomitable. The sense that they might be losing the race to another lab hung over them. Damadian was inserted inside Indomitable several more times with the same disappointing result. Oscar the phantom was put into the machine and readings taken of it. The signals were just fine. Meanwhile, hints were dropped to Minkoff with increasing frequency. Ah, Larry, why don't you go in? Larry, it won't hurt. Larry, you doing anything tonight? I've got an idea for you. Goldsmith was the most frequent, and most direct, hint-dropper: "Larry, get in the damned machine already." Minkoff's response was unprintable, and his resistance was increased by Goldsmith's taunting. Damadian, meanwhile, debated whether he should use his authority and simply order Minkoff into the machine.

On July 3, failing to solve the problems with the coil and beginning to buckle under the pressure, Minkoff walked up to Damadian and told him he'd go into the machine.

This time around Damadian had drawn up a long checklist of things that had to work—twenty or thirty different items—and he methodically went through the list. "It was like a countdown. I wanted to be sure that if it didn't work then I would know that all the components in the system were functioning properly. I didn't know that the first time. So if it didn't work this time, it would be much more discouraging. But I really thought it was going to work."

By contrast, Goldsmith, in one of his sullen moods, didn't even want to hang around for the Minkoff scan.

"Oh, come on, why don't you stick around?" Damadian said.

"It's never going to work," Goldsmith said.

"You want to bet?" Damadian asked.

"What do you bet?"

"I say it has a ninety percent chance of succeeding," Damadian said right back.

Goldsmith replied, "I say ten percent."

At almost the stroke of midnight, Minkoff took his shirt off. He raised his arms straight over his head, and the cardboard vest was slipped over his slender chest. It was still a fairly tight fit. If Minkoff exhaled heavily, his chest would brush against the coil. Minkoff sat down on the rail, looking somewhat like an escape artist buckled into a straitjacket. Satisfied that the antenna was properly positioned, Goldsmith and Damadian arranged themselves before the controls. There was a muteness about the lab. Damadian was swelling with exuberance, but he had been disappointed so many times before, he tried not to let it brim over. "So here was another step into the unknown. I was hoping it would work. I thought it would work. I was going to be more depressed this time if it didn't."

Looking from Minkoff, stationary and helpless in the machine, to Goldsmith, Damadian couldn't resist quipping, "Well, Mike, you've finally got Larry where you've wanted him all these years."

Everyone laughed.

As soon as the machine was flicked on, there was a signal. The rising excitement in the lab was palpable. Indomitable did work. Minkoff expected to be in the machine no more than a few minutes, because he thought the experiment would be a flop. But now there was no possibility that he would get that vest off quickly. "We saw that signal on the oscilloscope," Damadian said, "and we weren't about to let him out. It looked hopeful, but we still didn't know if we could get a scan, if it would focus as it had on Oscar and the turkey and give us an image.

"The focused spot was in the center. To move it, we had to move Larry. We had a graduate student at each end of the rail. I said, 'Move him to the right one inch.' They shoved. Then we recorded the data for a couple of minutes. Then I said, 'Move him another inch.' So we moved him inch by inch across the width of his whole chest. Then we moved him backward and forward. We knew after the first line scan, when there was signal in the heart, no signal in the lung, and then signal again after we got to his skin, that it was focusing. It was a real high for us. We were making history."

The process of recording information for the scan was laborious. A half hour, an hour went by. Minkoff was tiring. He was sitting there with his arms raised above his head, as if he were being held up at gunpoint, because if he let his arms drop he would louse up the impedance of the coil. Every so often his arms would start to droop and Goldsmith would bark at him to get them back up. When Minkoff exhaled, his chest would touch the coil and also foul up the signal, so every time a reading was taken, Minkoff had to hold his breath. After about an hour, with Minkoff noticeably weary, Damadian strung some rope across the front of Indomitable so Minkoff could drape his arms over it. His arms were going numb for the lack of circulation.

"I was in pain," Minkoff said. "And I was cold. It was chilly just sitting there." After two hours had lapsed, Damadian called for a break. Among others, the graduate students were bushed from pushing Minkoff back and forth. Minkoff went downstairs and got an ice-cream bar to restore some of his energy. Then it was back into Indomitable. The pain got worse. The cold. At three in the morning, Minkoff couldn't take the shivering any longer and he put his T-shirt back on. The graduate students, their energies flagging, wanted to quit and go home. They didn't realize a cardinal principle of science: If something's working, you don't quit. Who knew when it would be working again?

Goldsmith, turning the dials, was enormously excited. Nonetheless, he couldn't resist taunting the helpless Minkoff. If there was ever an opportunity to goad Minkoff, Goldsmith would seize it. Goldsmith would be taking his sweet time moving the focusing point through Minkoff's chest. Minkoff, aching, would say, "C'mon, Mike, hurry up, hurry up."

Goldsmith would adopt that impish grin of his and reply,

"Larry, watch this." And then he would move his hands in slow motion over the controls.

Minkoff would explode in rage. Damadian would say, "Calm down, calm down." Every time Minkoff moved, it would create distortions. Damadian was just hoping to complete an image without a rumble.

Minkoff stayed in Indomitable for four hours and forty-five minutes.

Minkoff's entire chest was done. The process had required moving him into sixty-four different positions. Some twenty to thirty signals were taken from each position and then averaged using a device known as a signal averager. As data were received, Goldsmith sketched out an image by hand with colored pencils on a sheet of graph paper. On a subsequent day they would feed the information into a computer to reconstruct a polished image. The picture Goldsmith drew showed a cross section through the chest, revealing the body wall, the right and left lungs, the heart (the right atrium and one of its ventricles), and a cut through the descending aorta. The image was normal. Minkoff would be relieved to know that he had no tumors.

"We were ecstatic," Damadian has said of the moment. "We'd done it—from the discovery of the diseased signal all the way to the first human scan. I thought my feet would never come back down to the ground. It was the most exciting thing in my life. It was the culmination of seven years of toil. Larry, Mike, and I could barely believe it had happened. And we knew it would have major impact on the scientific community. This was opening the human body to the world of the tissue molecule."

A jubilant Goldsmith scrawled in his notebook: "Conclusion: We have a great image!!"

Damadian had stashed away a bottle of white wine with which to celebrate the first human scan. He broke it out and

180

everyone had a swig. Damadian lit up his victory cigar and strutted around the lab, a wreath of smoke above him, the grin of a Cheshire cat on his face. They were all deliriously happy. The past now seemed all worth it. The legions of critics who had scoffed at them would be stilled. The believers —barely enough people to fill a small room—would be vindicated. At one point in the celebration, it occurred to Goldsmith that today was his wedding anniversary and he ought to get home at some point.

Though groggy with exhaustion, Damadian, Goldsmith, and Minkoff drove around for a while and talked about the scan. Damadian did not want to let Minkoff out of his sight. If anything was wrong with him after the nearly five hours inside the big magnet, Damadian would feel awful. He searched for the first indication that anything was awry. Though nothing other than extreme fatigue seemed evident, Damadian followed him home and waited patiently while he took a long shower, then insisted that Minkoff come over to his home and sleep on the couch. Though he personally harbored no worry, Minkoff agreed to do what Damadian asked. He seemed fine. "We were bone-tired," Damadian said. "We went to sleep. It was probably the most peaceful sleep of my life."

Despite being thoroughly wiped out by the night's happy events, Damadian squeezed in only a couple of hours of sleep. It was the Fourth of July, and every Independence Day his wife's family hosted a big picnic at their house in East Quogue. It was set on an expanse of well-coiffed land right on the bay. Around 120 people regularly attended, and there were three-legged races and pie-eating contests and a tug-of-war. Damadian gleefully went to the event, armed with the sketched picture of the Minkoff scan. He forced everyone he ran into to take a look at it, as if he were a proud father showing off baby pictures. "I'd never seen him quite so happy,"

Donna recalled. "He was showing everyone the picture and was happy as a lark."

The day after the momentous experiment, Damadian began work on a paper detailing the breakthrough, which he shortly thereafter submitted for publication to the obscure journal *Physiological Chemistry and Physics.* He deliberately bypassed the more promiment publications such as *Science* and *Nature,* because he didn't want to wait the months that it would have taken before it was published and afford his rivals a chance to break into print first. "It wouldn't have surprised me if one of the others had put together anything, even if it was a sack of potatoes, just to get published before me."

As Damadian worked on his paper, he was interrupted by thoughts of the wonder of what had happened. "This must have been what it felt like to step on the moon for the first time," he remarked. "Going someplace where no one has ever been before. It made my mind swim."

FOURTEEN

Nearly twenty reporters had gathered in the Downstate laboratory—more human beings than had ever been in the room. Some of them looked bored; others seemed expectant. Indomitable was the agenda item that had drawn the crowd.

Nervous that rival scientists would attempt to undermine his accomplishment, Damadian had immediately called a press conference to trumpet his news to the world. As it turned out, the regular publicity person for the university who had previously handled papers by him had recently left for another job. When Damadian approached the replacement, she said she was much too busy working on another project having to do with the social development of pregnant women. Thus Damadian had taken the unusual step of finding an outside publicity agent to orchestrate a news conference. Quite by chance, he hired Lawrence Penzell, president of Penzell Associates Inc., a Manhattan PR firm. In short order, he whipped up a release and invitation to the conference to be held on July 20, 1977, at ten in the morning. In the conventional manner of most PR hype, the somewhat confusing and misleading release read in part:

"FONAR's development came about in several stages. In 1971, the first experiment using cancer tissue in test tubes that had been surgically removed from normal tissue with respect to their radio signal emissions. One year later, in 1972, came the advent of Dr. Damadian's FONAR signal focusing, enabling cancer detection in the live person. Finally, in 1976 he brought about the first demonstration of tumor detection in the live mouse and the formulation of tumor images of this animal on a video monitor. This was followed by the construction of specially designed instrumentation for the rat; monkey; and finally, the introduction of more sophisticated equipment for human detection.

"After further experimentation, Dr. Damadian finally achieved a major medical break-through in cancer detection WITHOUT NECESSITATING X-RAY, NOR MAJOR SURGERY. Here, at this press conference, attendees will witness the application of this technique to the first live human being. The human subject will be introduced into this giant magnet for the scanning of his anatomy and the formation of the world's first image of living human organs on the video screen. . . .

"The FONAR invention, introduced at this conference, describes instrumentation capable of obtaining chemical data directly from any diseased organ without surgery. The chemical information so obtained is then formed as a video display on a color and/or black and white television screen. This gives birth to a major, new approach to the non-surgical detection of cancer without the ionizing radiation of X-ray with its main thrust continuing to be the visualization of tumors in the body. Additionally, it pinpoints a chemical characterization of the tumor which will permit determination not only of the type of tumor, but equally, how long it has existed; how widespread its metastases, [and] the extent of the malignancy and provide a rational basis for selecting the most appropriate chemical remedy. Ultimately, there is the prospect of a technique whereby the malignant radio signals could serve as target frequencies for aiming cancer destructive radiation at the tumor, to obliterate it without surgery."

The weather at the time was beastly hot, so Penzell arranged for a chartered bus to ferry reporters from the New York Public Library at 42nd Street and Fifth Avenue to the Downstate campus.

Little did the reporters boarding the bus that steamy morning know how close Damadian had come to a fiasco. Several days before, Minkoff had been finishing the task of inputting the data from the scan into the computer so that it could be reconstructed into an image; it was a tedious process, but it was necessary if Damadian was going to be able to show a video image. All he had had until that point was a hand-drawn picture. Joel Stutman showed up at the laboratory early that evening. The place was empty. Curious about whether any progress had been made on constructing the picture, Stutman sat down and turned on the computer. When he called up the image, he was astonished. It was finished, and it was beautiful to behold. "I could see everything—the heart, the lungs."

Wanting to share his joy, Stutman darted outside and, hearing noise down the hall, went looking for people. He found a graduate student in one of the other labs and grabbed hold of her arm and all but dragged her back with him. They reached the computer at nine thirty-four. It is possible to be that precise about time, because at that moment lightning bolts struck Consolidated Edison electrical transmission lines in northern Westchester, plunging the city into darkness.

The lights blinked off in the lab. The computer went out and the disk with the image was promptly and irretrievably wiped clean. Stutman stood there, in the dark, in sheer terror.

The next day, with power restored to the city, Stutman and Minkoff, drawing from the hand-scribbled data, began once again to feed the information into the computer. They worked practically nonstop. At eight o'clock on the morning of the press conference, barely in time, the image was re-created.

The reaction of the press was not altogether what Damadian had anticipated. Though keen interest was expressed by most of the members of the group, several reporters were notably hostile, in part perhaps because of the hyperbole of the Penzell release. Attendees were not, as had been implied, going to witness a person being scanned for the first time; they were going to see the Minkoff image and the ungainly machine that had produced it. "The first few questions were on the timid side," Koutcher said, "and then it got going and it was rather antagonistic." Koutcher, who was by nature rather cautious, thought that perhaps Damadian should have been a bit more restrained; he was uncomfortable, for instance, about the suggestion that the machine could lead to a method of destroying cancer tissue. "Damadian always had a penchant for claiming at least as much as he could and then some," Koutcher says. "If he wasn't sure if he had seventy cents in his pocket or ninety cents, he would say he had ninety cents. As Goldsmith once said, he gave himself the benefit of the doubt."

On that evening's telecast, Roger Field, the science editor of Channel 11 (WPIX-TV) noted, "Now at today's press conference Damadian seemed to be making some very extravagant claims." He then said that he had solicited some comments from experts in the field. Their reactions, offered under the cloak of anonymity, ran:

"If true, terrific. Needs more investigation."
"Cannot detect malignant tumors."
"Claims are premature and inflated."
"Doesn't publish his details."

The New York Times had assigned a staff reporter to cover the conference, and he wrote an article that appeared on page 18 of the following day's edition, under the headline NEW YORK RESEARCHER ASSERTS NUCLEAR MAGNETIC TECHNIQUE CAN DETECT CANCER, BUT DOUBTS ARE RAISED. The story began, "A New York City medical researcher announced yesterday at a news conference that he had developed 'a new technique for the nonsurgical detection of cancer anywhere in the human body.' However, in an interview later in the day, he retracted a contention that he had already used the technique on a cancer patient.

"And other cancer experts expressed skepticism that the technique had reached the stage where it could be used in diagnosing cancer."

The story went on to point out that Damadian had developed the technique while under a contract with the National Cancer Institute. It then noted that the federal agency was no longer supporting research into nuclear magnetic resonance and quoted Larry Blaser, an NCI spokesman, as saying, "We don't look on nuclear magnetic resonance as a promising area of diagnosis" in cancer. Farther on in the story, the reporter wrote: "Dr. Damadian said that he had approved a news release, also issued yesterday, prepared by Penzell Associates of 600 Third Avenue here, that contended that Dr. Damadian's Fonar technique 'is used to discover cancerous tissue in the live patient.'

"However, Dr. Damadian said at the news conference that he had not yet tested the device on a patient and had not yet documented that the device could detect a cancer in a human. When the inconsistency was pointed out at the news conference, Dr. Damadian said he stood by the news release.

"But later in the interview, after repeated questioning, Dr. Damadian said that he retracted as 'not accurate' the contention that his device had diagnosed cancer anywhere in the body. He expressed hope that it would do so someday.

"The news release also said that after studies on rats and monkeys, Dr. Damadian 'finally achieved a major medical breakthrough in cancer detection without necessitating X-ray, nor major surgery.'

"It further said that those attending the news conference would witness the 'application of the technique to the first live human being.' However, a reporter noted that the scan Dr. Damadian used for demonstration purposes was one done on one of his assistants and was dated July 3.

"The manner of Dr. Damadian's announcement was rather unusual. Ordinarily, researchers report their findings at a medical conference or through scientific journal articles. Sometimes, a medical center and its researchers hold a news conference in conjunction with publication of a journal article.

"Dr. Damadian called a news conference and sent out news releases without knowledge of Downstate Medical Center officials. However, after these officials were informed, they said that the news conference was 'legitimate' and that they stood behind the statement made in Dr. Damadian's news release.

"Dr. Damadian took the unusual step of retaining the Penzell Associates public relations and advertising firm and chartered a bus to bring representatives of the news media and financial institutions to Downstate Medical Center in New York."

Damadian left the lab the evening of the day that the *Times* story ran visibly agitated and somber. "When I read the *Times* article, I almost had apoplexy. That article really killed me. All the people who thought that I was crazy now had hard evidence. After that, people who were friends of mine would pass me in the hall and they wouldn't even talk to me. It was a very, very bad time for me. Very bad."

At home, he was uncommunicative. Sluggish and with no appetite, he moped about the house and stared gloomily at the walls. He felt the *Times* article had twisted what he said. He realized also that the press release was badly worded and he wondered how he had approved it, but in the craziness of what was going on, he must have. His wife tried to console him, not fully comprehending the depth of his dejection.

"It's only one newspaper article," she said. "Why are you so upset about one silly newspaper article?"

"It's more than one article," Damadian replied. "It's *The Times*. It will have a wide impact. People aren't going to believe what I've done."

Years ago, shortly after he joined the faculty of Downstate, Damadian had purchased a dilapidated house on 150 acres in Vermont, about fifteen miles from the Canadian border. He and Donna fixed it up and regularly went there for vacations. A garden was planted and they would eat its harvest; also, they had an antique buggy that they bought at an auction and they would rent a horse, attach it and frisk merrily about their property. That weekend the Damadians went up to Vermont and there was no joy. "He was depressed the whole time," Donna Damadian said. "He was quiet and distant. He was irritable. He didn't want to do things. I told him not to dwell on it so much. Just do what comes next and not dwell on the past. I thought he was overreacting. However, he thought it would keep him from getting a promotion and getting money and medical students."

Damadian, indeed, began to wonder seriously what, if anything, it would take for him to get some credit for his accomplishments. There was a rotating inner discomfort in him. After all the years of anguish and hard work, he had finally shown that you could probe the body with an NMR machine. He had done it and yet he still was no hero.

As word of the image spread throughout the scientfic community, however, congratulatory telegrams and letters began to trickle into Brooklyn, temporarily lifting Damadian's spirits.

"Delighted with your wonderful achievement," wrote Albert Szent-Gyorgyi, a Nobel laureate in biochemistry for his discovery of Vitamin C.

"Thank you very much for sending me a copy of your historic first picture," wrote E. M. Purcell, who had shared the Nobel for the discovery of NMR. "From a mouse and a hand to your beautiful chest cross section certainly is an impressive jump. I congratulate you and shall keep the picture as a perpetual reminder of how little one can foresee the fruitful applications of any new physics."

From the University of Nottingham came three letters. "Your progress is impressive. There are probably a few people suffering from envy now," wrote Waldo Hinshaw. "This is an important achievement and a valuable step forward in applying NMR imaging to medicine," wrote E. R. Andrew. And Peter Mansfield wrote, "Let me congratulate you on a very nice piece of work."

"It is clear that this is an advance of great promise and you are to be congratulated for your perseverance and pioneering skill in bringing it off so successfully," wrote A. K. Solomon, from the biophysical laboratory at the Harvard Medical School.

Elsewhere, though, Damadian's achievement was already being mercilessly picked apart. Digs from some of the competing laboratories had the distinct and predictable flavor of sour grapes. To many of his rivals, at least in any public pronouncements, the scan was depicted as amounting to little more than a meaningless stunt. Minkoff said, "After that news conference, you'd think all the sour grapes would stop. That just made it worse. A lot of people didn't believe it. They didn't want to believe it. What we did took a lot of people by surprise. That's what we always did. It's always been our nature to work in secret toward a goal and then when we accomplish it to spring it on people like a bomb."

"After we did the scan, our work became more controversial," Goldsmith said. "I submitted a number of papers and they were rejected. It came down to the fact that it was too hot for the journals to handle politically. After the image, things became worse in a number of ways. At first the criticism started to coalesce around the argument that, yes, you can determine the difference between cancerous tissue and normal tissue, but that's not the question. The question is, Can you determine the difference between cancerous tissue and other abnormal pathologies? There was very little data by anyone on this. Well, my feeling is you have to start on the ground floor. The ground floor was whether you could determine the difference between cancerous and normal tissue. I think there was a lot of resistance from the pathologists who had a vested interest in the current technology. They didn't want anything new unless it was handed to them in final form on a platter. As soon as we knocked down one objection they came up with another. Academicians in a sense are a lot like lawyers—not that lawyers aren't my favorite people. Very often they view their role in society as shooting holes in an idea rather than coming up with an honest test of the idea. They were saying that NMR was not one hundred percent accurate and pathology was one hundred percent, which is not true anyway. My response was that, well, why don't we all lie down and die. If science is so perfected that nothing can be added to it then there should be no research."

Eight years later, when I asked his reaction to the image, Paul Lauterbur said, "I wouldn't want to be quoted. Well, let's see if I could tone it down. The technique itself was an obvious dead end. It was slow and produced low resolution and poorly defined images. The magnet he built did not seem appropriate for that purpose. To build a low-field superconducting magnet seemed not a reasonable choice. He could have used a resistive magnet. . . . This is not the right way to do it, but it will get a lot of publicity. To a scientist, it's of no use. To the extent that someone is concerned about publicity and firsts, one would have hoped that things would have gone otherwise. If you're doing honest scientific research and someone else is doing the same thing and doing a good job of it and reaches that goal before you, that's when one feels the impact of that scientific competition."

Wasn't it important that Damadian proved that a big enough magnet could be built to produce a human image? I asked.

He replied, "There seemed to be no problem there. It was just a question of getting everything together at once. Like giving a diagram of a car. It's just not a question of whether the car would work. It's just a question of whether it would weigh one ton or five or cost twenty-five thousand dollars or fifty thousand dollars. These are just matters of detail."

He went on, "Those who had looked into it carefully believed it could be done. There was no question that the basic thing would work. It's like seeing a mountain in the distance. You're sure you can get there. You don't know whether you'll stumble over a four-lane highway or have to hack your way through the woods. But there's no question that you'll reach the mountain."

Donald Hollis attacked the breakthrough from a different point of view. When I asked him about it, he said, with an obvious tinge of displeasure, "It was nothing but a publicity stunt. Anyone could have done it. Paul Lauterbur could have done it. He said, 'Let's get a really good image of an animal, instead of some blob.' It wasn't useful. It wasn't good. It wasn't anything." He laughed, then said, "It's not good enough to even be sure it's human. I don't recognize it as a picture. I claim he did not take a picture of the human body."

Jason Koutcher, inordinately impressed by the Minkoff image, showed it to a couple of friends of his who were medical students. He didn't tell them what it was. They recognized it right off as a human chest.

When Don Vickers was asked for his sense of the NMR

community's reaction to Damadian's scan, he excused himself for a moment while he fumbled for a piece of paper buried in the clutter on his desk, then, upon finding it, read off a favorite quotation of his from Machiavelli's *The Prince:* "It must be remembered that there's nothing more difficult to plan, more doubtful of success, nor more dangerous to manage than the creation of a new system. For the initiator has the enmity of all who would profit by the preservation of the old institution and merely lukewarm defenders in those who would gain by the new ones."

FIFTEEN

There was no time for Damadian and his team to lounge around and savor their achievement. They were convinced that the crude Indomitable was the first step to a human scanner. But plenty of work stood before them if a true commercial machine was to be developed.

The next challenge was to get the scan time down. There was obviously no value in a scanner that required a patient to remain imprisoned inside it for close to five hours. A key reason it took so long was the horrendous signal-to-noise ratio. In the weeks following the first scan, Goldsmith struggled with the problem. After some manipulation of the electronics, he felt he had achieved discernible improvements, and so Minkoff went back into the coil on July 18.

Minkoff was even more reluctant than he had been the first time. He was genuinely worried about his health. He had been feeling ill recently and thought it might be due to an allergy. He was allergic to cats, but he hadn't been around any cats. After he had a blood test done, a minor condition was revealed—an abnormal white count—and although there was no reason to link that to his experience in Indomitable, he was concerned. But he went back into the machine, and Damadian and Goldsmith successfully, and somewhat more quickly, recorded his heart, lung, and left pectoral muscle.

A few days later, Damadian felt encouraged enough to attempt to scan a cancer patient. The subject chosen was a man named Jim Southard, someone Damadian knew from his Forest Hills church. He had a tumor very high up in his chest, almost in his neck. He knew he was dying and several times implored Damadian to scan him in his new invention. The outcome was a total failure; no image at all resulted.

Clearly, significant improvement needed to be achieved in the signal-to-noise ratio. Damadian thought the answer might be a shielded room to block out extraneous noise and so a chamber made out of laminated flakeboard and galvanized metal was purchased and installed in October. The signal-to-noise ratio was still awful.

At this point, a dearth of money put Indomitable into hibernation. Not only did Damadian lack any future working capital but he was forty thousand dollars in the hole. He owed half the amount to his department for an image-display system he had bought. During the process of building Indomitable, Damadian had no display system on which to show an image other than the primitive device he had used for the mouse that made images in rectangles rather than tiny dots. He implored the department chairman, Alfred Bollet, for money, promising to pay him back with forthcoming grants. The forthcoming grants never came, and now the chairman wanted the debt repaid.

The balance of Damadian's indebtedness was for liquid helium, a constant drain on his bankroll, like a mortgage to a laid-off worker. As Damadian would grumble, "It was costing me a hundred thousand dollars a year to feed the dinosaur."

Sympathy for Damadian was not in much abundance at Downstate, since his star had not risen very much after the historic experiment. "I was still perceived throughout the university as a wild man. Imagine this guy on the fifth floor who was knocking down walls and putting holes in the ceiling and building big magnets that are going to pull the fillings out of everybody's teeth. You go up there at night and he's pouring smoke into it. All I needed was a grin on my face and I would've been a good facsimile of a Charles Addams character."

The injustices from elsewhere in the scientific world didn't seem to end either. Right after he had gotten the first human image, Damadian had notified the *Medical Tribune* in London, thinking that the paper might care to carry a story on the breakthrough. No, he was told by an editor, it didn't sound especially newsworthy. In the December 5, 1977, issue of the *Medical Tribune,* Damadian was aghast to read a story headlined: NEW BODY SCAN TECHNIQUE GIVES PICTURES IN LIVING COLOR. Datelined Nottingham, it began, "A noninvasive technique for producing pictures of the interior of the human body—with almost textbook anatomical detail—has been achieved by biomedical researchers here. The technique, which uses a strong magnetic field, holds great promise in the diagnosing and treatment of cancer." The story went on to elaborate on work presented at a scientific meeting by Peter Mansfield. The story said that Mansfield's team had "produced cross-sectional pictures of tissue water distribution through a human head and body." The clear implication was that the British group had produced the first images by NMR scanning. Mansfield had in fact shown hand-drawn simulations of what an NMR image might look like, basing the drawings on X-rays of autopsy specimens.

"It was outrageous," Damadian said bitterly. "Here I had produced an actual chest image, and he was getting publicity for some drawings from X-rays."

Not until Christmas Eve of 1977, as a belated Christmas present, did Mansfield receive his human-sized magnet, months after it was expected. ("I still remember it," Mansfield told me. "Who wouldn't remember it? I was the only one in the department. Everyone else was at parties. I helped unpack the damned thing.") In April 1978, in forty minutes, a successful image was obtained of Mansfield's abdomen (he chose that part of the anatomy because Damadian had already laid claim to the chest)—the world's second human image, a picture that can be seen today tacked on the wall of Mansfield's office. Had "the bloody magnet arrived sooner," Mansfield felt he and not Damadian would have gotten the first scan. He was taken aback when he heard that Damadian had accomplished so much so quickly. "The effort he put in was monumental," he says. "You have to admire the guy. He set his mind to it and he pulled it off. Anyone who builds a magnet, especially a supercon, must be an unusual man."

Alfred Bollet didn't much care what Damadian had done or was doing; he wanted his twenty thousand dollars. He also wanted Damadian to pay his phone bill, which had crept into thousands of dollars. Formerly the department had paid it, but Bollet had changed the policy; now the scientists were expected to foot their own bills.

When no money arrived from Damadian, Bollet sent a letter on November 15, 1977, to Janet Halpern, the telecommunications coordinator for Downstate, that read simply: "Dear Janet: Please disconnect the following telephone extensions as soon as possible: 2410, 1586, 1558, 1559. Thank you for your assistance." Those were Damadian's extensions. With his phones cut off, Damadian felt slightly ridiculous. Long-distance calls were coming in from important scientists around the world. Sorry, they were told, that number is no longer a working number at the university. Fortunately, Damadian had a sympathetic friend in the telephone room who would periodically turn his phone back on. Bollet would find out and shut if off. On again. Off again.

Before Damadian was physically thrown out, some emergency grant money arrived and his debt was paid. "So I was eventually able to climb out of the hole. I narrowly avoided getting kicked out of my lab. I heard you would show up one day and your stuff would be out in the hall and a new lock on the door and you would have to go sit in the library. They couldn't boot me out of the university altogether, because I had tenure. If I didn't have tenure, I would have been fired and there would have been no Indomitable. Tenure saved my neck."

At this time, Damadian came up for promotion to full professor. "The people who were to rule on it said they couldn't judge the pictures we had made," Damadian said. "Then the *Times* article came out and that did it. I didn't get a promotion. I remained an associate professor and will until I die. The promotion would have given me more staff and money and opportunity. In retrospect, it drove me out of the university. If *The Times* hadn't written its article, I might be a full professor back at the university still doing nothing."

With Indomitable shut down, Goldsmith continued his work on cutting down the noise by using a small electric magnet in the lab, powering it off a twelve-volt car battery. Near Christmas, the team was satisfied enough with their progress that Damadian decided to charge up the human magnet. There did indeed seem to be significant improvement in the signal-to-noise ratio, and thus Oscar, the senior phantom, was put into the coil to be scanned. The scan was a flop. They theorized that the shielded room contained steel that conducted magnetic forces and thus increased the size of the focusing spot on Indomitable.

The room was dismantled and replaced by a substitute that the group built themselves out of nonmagnetic materials. That was completed by the end of January, whereupon Oscar Jr. was successfully imaged. A scan was completed of Minkoff in an hour and forty-five minutes, a sharp improvement in time. On February 1, another image was done of Minkoff that was achieved in just thirty-eight minutes. After some more pictures were taken of Nean Hu and then of the calf of Damadian's leg, another cancer patient was brought in, Sou Chan,

Damadian's sister's father-in-law and the owner of Manhattan's House of Chan restaurant. On February 5, he was successfully scanned, thus producing the first image of cancer in a human being. He had a terrible cancer that showed up all over the image. Minkoff then immediately went into the machine so they could compare the scan to that of a healthier person.

By now it seemed likely to Damadian that an NMR scanner could be sold to someone. Clear interest, in fact, was sparking up in corporate quarters. Looking for money, Damadian had approached a wealthy acquaintance in Forest Hills who had made his fortune by developing a motorized crane designed to work on the back of barges. Among the companies he had business dealings with was General Electric. When Damadian talked to him about his invention, the man said, "Why, you really ought to see the GE people." "But they'll steal my idea," Damadian said. "No, don't worry about that," he was assured. The man contacted someone he knew at GE, and before long an executive in the company's medical systems division called Damadian and arranged to visit his Downstate lab. Damadian demonstrated Indomitable for the executive, who expressed polite interest. Damadian never heard from GE again. Not long afterward, word trickled down to him that GE was revving up its engines to embark on the development of an NMR scanner.

The December 1977 issue of *Popular Science* magazine featured a cover story on Damadian's supermagnet. Shortly afterward, Damadian received a phone call from a Johnson & Johnson vice-president. He said his son read *Popular Science* and had shown the story to him, since he thought the company might well be interested in the invention. Could they come down and take a peek?

In early 1978 the vice-president and his entourage paid a visit to Downstate, were apparently suitably impressed, and asked Damadian if he would like to join the company. The company would probably form a new subsidiary and install Damadian as its head. Damadian said, sure, he was interested. Meanwhile, the Johnson & Johnson people poked around to see who else was working in the NMR field, interviewed some rivals, and decided after some deliberation that Waldo Hinshaw was their man.

Damadian shrugged off the rejection. "By this time," he said, "we had a real flying machine. All he had was a model airplane."

On April 4, 1978, the Downstate team did a scan of Nean Hu's wrist and then of Damadian's wrist. This was several months after Hinshaw had published an image of a wrist using his sensitive point technique, which was quite good and proved important in showing how detailed an image was possible using NMR. Damadian was impressed with the quality and wanted to see how an Indomitable image compared. It didn't. "That's when we realized," Goldsmith said, "that we were still very much in a race."

Before any further images could be made, funds again ran completely dry, making it impossible to buy helium to cool the magnet. Damadian's work ground to a standstill.

One morning shortly after he had shut down Indomitable for what looked like the last time, Damadian was sitting in his office doodling. Money problems were more impossible than ever. The department didn't seem to care at all about what he was doing. It appeared that no matter what he did, he was mocked as openly as ever. He longed to get out of the university. Returning to a thought that had been at the back of the minds of the team for some time, Damadian seriously considered starting a company. Goldsmith, Minkoff, and Stutman needed little convincing.

"The goal was to make enough money to do the research we wanted to do without being constrained to write grant requests and satisfy the peer-review committees," Goldsmith said. "I wanted to be rich enough to do the research I wanted to do and to be left alone. I think that that was Damadian's goal also.

"After the patent we intended to go into business based on that patent. The intention was to bring this stuff to some sort of commercial utility. At least that was my intent. I'm not sure that was Damadian's motivation. Damadian's intention right from the start was to cure disease. He wanted to make an important humanitarian contribution. I can't say that I shared that. I'd certainly rather make a humanitarian contribution than not make a humanitarian contribution. If I had to say what my prime motivation was, though, it was financial. When Damadian and I had disagreements, they would be along those lines."

Damadian made a phone call and sounded out Bill Akers, his Nashville rescuer, about the idea. Akers's blunt advice was to forget it. "I discouraged him," Akers said later. "I thought raising the money and so forth would be an inordinate obstacle."

But Damadian was persistent. How much would it take? Akers had a friend who was an executive at Texas Instruments, and, figuring he could make as reasonable a guess as anyone he knew, Akers had him fly up from Dallas to take a look at Damadian's situation. Akers greeted him at the airport, and they drove over to Downstate. On the way there, the Texan said, "Bill, I know something about NMR and I just don't think this guy can do what he says he can." Akers urged the man just to wait and see.

When Damadian got around to asking what kind of money it might take to get a company off the ground, the Texan looked around, shifted his weight, and said he guessed he would probably need two million dollars. According to Akers's memory of the episode, "It was just a curbstone opinion. He didn't really know if it would take five million dollars or twenty million dollars to start that company. So my friend went back to Texas. Raymond thought the two million dollars was a reachable goal, and so he set out to raise it. If my friend had said twenty million dollars, which he might well have said, then Raymond would have probably forgotten about starting some company."

When he was not selling insurance and homes, David Terry was on the lookout for ways to raise money for Damadian. He was well known on the ritzy eastern end of Long Island among the well-to-do who summered there. One day quite by accident he met a man in Westhampton who was a professional "finder," a member of that odd fraternity of individuals who round up money for others in return for a cut of the action. I will call him Harry Larkin.

"I met him out at a rental and took a liking to him," Terry told me. "I used to stop by while I was a cop and have tea with him. In the course of these sessions, he told me he was a professional fund-raiser. He seemed to make oil deals out West. So I mentioned Raymond to him and he said, gee, I ought to be raising money for him." One night, Terry took him into Brooklyn and introduced him to Damadian. "I met him," Damadian told me, "and he was all eager to help us raise millions to start our business. If you ever meet one of these guys, they talk about the sky raining hundred-dollar bills and they can't keep up with all the money. What did I know? I was gullible. I believed he could raise millions."

Damadian signed a contract with Larkin. According to its terms, Larkin was to raise two million dollars within a year's time. As a precaution, Damadian added that he had to produce six hundred thousand dollars in six months or the contract would be nullified. In return, Larkin would get a 10 percent stake in the new company. Damadian relaxed and waited for the shower of gold that would transform his life.

Over the ensuing weeks, Larkin would periodically bring potential investors out to Downstate to visit the labs and meet Damadian. Out of his earshot, though, Larkin would refer to Damadian as "the crazy professor." Six months lapsed and Larkin hadn't raised a dime. He pleaded for an extension. Some deals were cooking. It would just be a matter of time before the money started pouring in. "You could never tell if he was telling the truth," Terry says. "He was a bullshit artist." Forget it, Damadian told him. Incensed, Larkin threatened to sue, though he never did. He simply vanished. As Damadian puts it, "He came like the wind. He went like the wind."

In March 1978, Damadian conceived a name, the FONAR Corporation, for his penniless company. He was ready to incorporate. Freeman Cope had told him about a book that explained how you could incorporate your own business for fifty dollars or less. So Damadian obtained a copy of the book, tore out a form that was included in it, wrote out a check for fifty dollars, and sent it off to the author. As routinely as that, FONAR came into existence. With Larkin now completely out of the picture, Damadian summoned double-duty Terry and told him that it would be up to the two of them to round up the money to capitalize the company.

"Great," Terry thought. "Just what I needed. I didn't know what a stock was, what a warrant was. I had had a lot of practice at flea markets, but that was about it."

A goal was set to attempt to raise two and a half million dollars from private individuals. Damadian and Terry put together a list of people who they thought might cough up the money. They decided to sell blocks of fifty thousand dollars and they would take whatever help they could get. Danny

Culver, Terry's plumber cousin, tried to sell FONAR while he was out repairing leaky pipes in Long Island's cavernous South Shore mansions. "He would go out with an assistant," Terry explained. "The assistant would do the plumbing and Danny talked FONAR." Meanwhile, Terry was calling on everyone he had ever met during his days selling real estate and from his experiences on the police force. Someone he had once given a speeding ticket to would now become a prospect for some FONAR stock. In the most haphazard way, nibbles started to occur.

It was not until July 1978, though, that Terry had a score. "This guy came into my agency one day and we talked about the sale of a gun. We shook hands and he walked out my office door. I had a thought. I got up and said, 'John, you have a minute, can I show you something?' He said sure. I showed him some tapes of Frank Field [then WNBC-TV science reporter] interviewing Raymond on TV. He just watched silently. He was clearly shocked. He said he was going to talk to his father and his brothers. A day later, he called and wanted his wife and father to see the tapes. I went over to his house and ran them again. They watched them and they were just amazed."

John Campagna was the man Terry showed the tape to that summer day in his agency office. Campagna's family was in the real estate and building business. "I took a trip to the lab in the city with Campagna, his brother, David, and his father, John," Terry said. "There was garbage all over. It was kind of unbelievable. It was really an unpleasant place to be in. How anyone could do any work in it, no less meaningful work, was beyond me. But that machine was something. And Damadian was impressive. The next day, they said, 'We're in for fifty thousand.'"

David Campagna remembers visiting the lab and having not the faintest understanding of the technology they were hearing about. "But Raymond's enthusiasm is what did it. The guy was incredibly enthusiastic. So we believed him."

After a tour of the lab, Damadian suggested lunch. He took the Campagnas to a pizza place across the street from Downstate. It was certainly one of the worst restaurants—possibly the worst—they had ever eaten in. Damadian did most of the talking, and they continued to listen raptly to all that he said. The elder Campagna said that they would be pleased to invest in the venture.

Driving back to Long Island, David Campagna, a little perplexed by the suddenness of it all, said to his father, "But there's no agreement or anything? We just send in a check?"

His father turned and looked at him and said slowly, "Well, sometimes you just have to do business this way."

Over the next couple of years, the Campagna family bought something like six hundred thousand dollars' worth of FONAR stock.

The first person Damadian approached was Bill Judson. He bumped into him while he was looking for Ken Judson, Bill's brother. Judson owned Hollowick Inc., which made Hollowick lamps, atmospheric lights that resemble old-fashioned oil lamps and are commonly found in diners and restaurants. "Ken Judson was a kid I grew up with. I knew he and his brother had inherited a good amount of money from their father. Ken Judson also was a successful Wall Street investment banker. So I went to the tennis club one day looking for Ken. I ran into his brother, Bill, in the locker room. I told Bill what I wanted to talk to Ken about, a business idea. He said he'd like to hear about it, and so I had lunch with him. When I was done, he said he'd like to put fifty thousand dollars into that right away. He'd have a check in a week. I was stunned. I had written Kerkorian and others with millions and I had gotten nothing. That was our first check. I subsequently talked to Ken, but he wanted no part of FONAR. Too risky, he said."

Encouraged by these early strikes, Terry and Damadian pushed on. Terry said, "We got to know by someone's occupation whether he would buy stock or not. Most of the people who invested in FONAR initially were self-made men who took risks or had danger in their lives. Guys who were ex-airline pilots or cops came in." Among the people Terry called on were members of the family that owned the lumberyard he had worked in years ago. They invested. One Quogue investor who bought a fifty-thousand-dollar block brought a suit-case stuffed with twenty-, fifty-, and hundred-dollar bills. He didn't trust banks. Neither Terry nor Damadian had ever seen that much money in cash. By the time Terry and Damadian had finished their rounds, a not insignificant proportion of Westhampton Beach had tied up its money in the fortunes of the FONAR Corporation.

Money had been raised among some thirty-five individuals. The turndown rate was surprisingly low. Damadian once calculated that 80 percent of the people who bothered to come and see Indomitable bought a block of stock. "The super-wealthy invariably turned us down. A Greek shipping billionaire turned us down. He analyzed it and analyzed it. His attorney ultimately said no." Twenty percent of the company was sold to outside investors. Damadian himself put up fifty thousand dollars. He had about ten thousand saved. He sold his house and arranged for a larger mortgage on another house and borrowed the rest. "I wanted everybody to know that if they lost their money, I would lose mine, too. I didn't have a dime left."

It seemed prudent to Damadian to accumulate at least six hundred thousand dollars, enough to really get the company off the ground, before spending any. But Bill Judson insisted that he get cracking and at least spend some of Bill's money right away. In June, he went and found Damadian an appropriate space to rent out in Plainview, Long Island. Damadian was interested in a site that was convenient to Downstate but beyond the border of Queens, so that he wouldn't have to pay New York City taxes. The place was five thousand square feet. "When we walked in," Damadian said, "it was more space than I had ever seen in my life. I was going to have all this space and pay rent and assume responsibility. It scared me half to death."

Damadian was jittery. He was a scientist, not a businessman. He had a dream, and his dream stood before him in crude metal form. Whether he could turn that into something sleek and reliable and get hospitals to shell out hundreds of thousands of dollars for it, he had no idea. As was his custom any time he got scared, he did what seemed to be the only thing to do. He plowed forward.

When they moved into Plainview, Damadian, Minkoff, Goldsmith, and Joel Stutman opened up a bridge table and folding chairs, made themselves as comfortable as was possible given the makeshift circumstances, and, with a certain nervous optimism, planned the company. It had been decided that Damadian would be apportioned 51 percent of the company's stock, Minkoff and Goldsmith would each get 7 percent, and Stutman would receive 3.5 percent. Twenty percent had been sold to the thirty-five investors, and another 11.5 remained for future sale to backers.

The first order of business was where to place Minkoff and Goldsmith so that there would be a minimum of combustion. The solution that drew unanimous support was to put them in offices at opposite ends of the building. The next item on the agenda was to purchase equipment. They started to make out orders using the FONAR company name, but then it was decided that it might be wiser not to let Technicare and General

Electric know that they had formed a company. GE and Technicare knew the FONAR name well by now. "To give ourselves some peace," Damadian said, "we decided to use a code name. We were casting about for names when Joel Stutman said, 'Just spell FONAR backward.' I said, 'Joel, that's Ranof. What will our shareholders think about that?' So we made it Raanex." For two years, the company would operate under the name Raanex II Corporation until it came out of its cocoon with its first product.

Even before the company was formally founded, Damadian had made a crucial decision that if proved wrong could have cost the company its life. He decided to scrap the idea of building a commercial scanner with a superconducting magnet and instead attempt to build a permanent magnet big enough to pull out NMR signals. His reasoning was that a superconducting magnet was entirely too much trouble for hospitals to bother with. It was costly to run. Liquid helium and liquid nitrogen had to be purchased in never-ending quantities. Personnel had to be kept on staff just to feed the magnet its diet of coolants. It didn't make sense.

What made sense about a permanent magnet is hard to say. No one had ever built one as large as Damadian would need. Not many people thought one ever could be built. But the more he thought about the permanent magnet the more he felt that anything else would eventually become a white elephant. As he liked to say, "Henry Ford once said, 'I don't care how good your product is, if you can't sell it, it's not worth the powder to blow it up.'"

Bill Akers, who was among those privy to the decision on a permanent magnet, recalled his reaction to the idea: "I said, 'Why, Raymond, you just got a picture, the only picture in the world, and you did it with a superconducting magnet. Now you're going to change to a whole new ballgame.' And far as I saw, he was going to start all over. I thought it was an unwise idea. I made my living in a fairly practical field, so this didn't make much sense to me. The thing is, because he built that superconducting magnet with his own hands, he knew the problems that the magnet had. He saw that it would never be feasible for a doctor or a nurse in a clinic to run it, and that's where he envisioned its use. So he decided to go for it."

Methodical, silent, and intense, Damadian sat engrossed at his desk in his new quarters, steadfastly working out a design for a permanent magnet. He began on the puzzle in early October 1978. Within a couple of weeks, he had produced a signal from a small model. He won't say how he made the magnet, for fear that competitors will steal the idea. Minkoff, meanwhile, was designing a bed for the machine, on which a patient would lie while he was scanned. Goldsmith worked on the coil. Once he had completed the small prototype, Damadian started building a larger one. At four-thirty in the morning on December 19, he put the finishing touches on a five-hundred-gauss permanent magnet. He christened it Jonah. It marked the birth of permanent-magnet NMR scanning.

For the outside shell, or canopy, of the machine, Damadian knew he needed some cosmetics. Aesthetics matter, even in medical detection equipment. Until then, Damadian couldn't have cared less about looks, but he wanted a modern appearance, not some boxy shape. Fiberglas seemed the appropriate material, since Fiberglas molds are cheap. Friends told him to get in touch with Pratt Institute in Brooklyn which boasts one of the country's best industrial design departments, and to try to line up the services of an industrial designer. Damadian mulled the advice over and decided that what he really needed was a sculptor. "I decided it had to be an Italian sculptor, because I had been very impressed when I was in Italy by the Italian artisans."

He phoned Pratt and asked for the chairman of the industrial design department. He was delighted to discover that his
name was Orelli.

"I need to find an Italian sculptor," he told the chairman,
briefly explaining his task.

"That's going to be tough," was the reply. "But I'll look
around."

A week later, the chairman called back and said, "What
about the son of an Italian sculptor?"

"I'll take him," Damadian said.

Robert Pirelli (not his real name) reported for work almost
immediately. He was given a briefing on what was needed
and began fabricating clay models of possible shells for the
scanner. It took him a full year to perfect a design.

It required a wealth of patience on Damadian's part to keep
him around. "He turned out to be crazy as a bedbug," Damadian said.

But he designed a gorgeous shell.

The next problem was to move the considerable distance
from a model to a full-sized canopy. As it happened, Damadian's sister had a sister-in-law who had recently married a
General Motors executive. One day, Damadian was chatting
with him about the canopy.

"No problem," he said. "I'll have some GM people do it for
you. I would say they could build the first mold for you for a
hundred and fifty thousand dollars."

Damadian was aghast. That was practically all the money in
the budget.

Damadian, of course, was a practiced hand at finding pinch-
penny means to ends. He had heard that boat builders on
Long Island made boats out of Fiberglas, and he thought that
perhaps they could also make a shell for an NMR scanner. So
Damadian journeyed out to the Patchogue boatyards to see a
boat builder named Ed Stillwagon, who he had been told was

remarkably versatile. Among other things, he once built a white Fiberglas desk for Johnny Carson that was used on *The Tonight Show.* Damadian outlined the situation and showed him the design.

"So do you think you could build me a canopy?"

"Why, sure."

"How much would it cost?"

"Would six thousand dollars be all right?"

Three months later, Stillwagon delivered the finished mold. It arrived at the FONAR offices on the back of a truck.

Extensive refinement of the electronics was necessary, and it was not until the fall of 1979 that the first good image was produced by the new machine. It was of David Terry's chest. Everyone was quite jubilant. As a gesture of his enthusiasm, David Terry's father made a hooked rug in the pattern of the image, and it was hung ceremoniously on the wall behind Damadian's desk. T-shirts were ordered with the image printed on them, as well, and everyone in the company started wearing them. Joel Stutman proudly donned his while playing golf.

By March 1980, the machine for commercial sale was complete. Raanex officially became known as the FONAR Corporation. The QED 80, as the first commercial NMR scanner was called, looked like a sleek mobile home that had had a hole gnawed out of the center of it by some large rodent, or like a doughnut that had been stepped on by a giant. A patient being scanned lay on what resembled a stretcher and entered the hole of the doughnut by computer control. Radio energy was fired at the patient through an antenna embedded in the plastic hood. He heard the grating of magnetic coils but felt nothing. When the radio energy was turned off, the antenna picked up the radio signals emitted by the body tissue and conveyed them to a computer, which analyzed them and depicted the result in pictorial form on a screen. The computer would make picture after picture of different "slices" of the body. The computer was also capable of analyzing the speed at which the nuclei returned to their original alignment, thus furnishing additional data about the environment and chemical composition of the tissue.

In April 1980, a prototype of the QED 80 was trucked to Las Vegas and unloaded at the MGM Grand Hotel, where it was launched upon the world at the annual meeting of the American Roentgen Ray Society, a significant radiological show. Damadian took along a selection of images, including a rather nice one of Joel Stutman's chest and a terrific image of Donna Damadian's liver. Naive to the ways of the business world, he went to the show fearful that he would be overwhelmed with orders for his miraculous invention and be unable to fulfill them quickly enough. So he kept the images in his jacket pocket and showed them selectively. To prepare for the stampede of orders, he had also had an emergency sales phone installed in his office ("I wanted it to be red, but I took black") so that the regular circuits wouldn't become overloaded. Two weeks lapsed before it rang. Damadian was several hundred yards away and galloped to his office to answer it. It was a wrong number.

In order to stimulate sales, four prototypes of the QED 80 were built. By the end of the year, one was placed at the radiologic diagnostic center of Dr. Ronald Ross in Cleveland, Ohio, where it was put to work on breast-cancer detection. Within the next year, the others were installed in the diagnostics radiology department at the University of Mexico in Monterrey, at the University of Milan in Italy, and at the Mochida Pharmaceutical Company in Japan, where they began to find immediate application, primarily for studies of the head. A price of five hundred and fifty thousand dollars was established for the scanner. Anyone who bought it, though, could use it only for clinical tests, since it had not yet received the blessings of the Food and Drug Administration. In June 1981, FONAR went public at an offering price of five dollars a share. The stock was immediately snapped up.

SIXTEEN

Any new technology inspires innovators to work from fresh perspectives that make the pioneers vulnerable to attack. The original development can quickly be made obsolete by subsequent strokes of brilliance. Little more than a year after he had thrust his QED 80 upon the world, Damadian was studying a set of pictures that made him sick. With their remarkable detail and clear resolution, they were almost too good to believe. But there was no denying them. At the 1981 meeting of the Radiological Society of North America, the biggest radiological show in the world, held at Chicago's McCormick Place, a company called Diasonics had on display at its booth stunning head and body images from its new thirty-five-hundred-gauss superconducting machine. They vastly outclassed FONAR's. Damadian had no idea such fabulous images were possible, and they awoke in him not only despondency but a sense of panic. FONAR, on which his whole identity had come to depend, was clearly (and so soon) imperiled. "We may be dead," he thought. "My baby may be dead."

It was a new world. Substantial companies and aggressive entrepreneurs, armed with sizable resources, had been bestirred and were plowing into NMR, determined to stake a claim in what was promising to blossom into a multibillion-dollar industry. Diasonics was a Milpitas, California, company founded in 1978 to make computer-driven ultrasound equipment that used sound waves to allow doctors to see images of some of the body's organs. To get into NMR, it had joined forces with a research team headed by Leon Kaufman, a physicist, and Lawrence Crooks, an electrical engineer, at the Radiologic Imaging Laboratory at the University of California at San Francisco. The group had done extensive research with a powerful NMR scanner, using an imaging technique known as two-dimensional Fourier transform that had first been demonstrated in 1975 by R. R. Ernst and fellow researchers at the Swiss Federal Institute of Technology and then further refined at the University of Aberdeen.

A half-dozen or so different methods, very different from Lauterbur's and Damadian's original methods, had emerged for converting NMR signals into cross-sectional images of living bodies. They varied in the ways they applied a magnetic field, isolated points within it, and collected and compiled NMR signals. Damadian himself would soon switch to the two-dimensional Fourier technique. The more powerful Diasonics magnet was able to achieve a far better signal-to-noise ratio. The hard work by the California team had paid off with the fabulous pictures that Diasonics now had to show. The images made it clear to everyone else in the fledgling field that in order to remain competitive it was necessary to go to higher-powered magnets.

Damadian considered these new and unanticipated circumstances. He quickly concluded that if he was going to rescue his company he had to produce a machine boasting a permanent magnet with a field of at least three thousand gauss. That large a magnet had never been built before. Most experts thought it impossible. The sudden decision split apart the company. In fact, virtually everyone but Damadian was staunchly opposed to the idea. They thought they should try to fiddle around with the five-hundred-gauss magnet to improve the images it produced; they argued that there was a galaxy of possibilities that they had not even begun to explore. "Just about everyone in the whole company was against this,"

Stutman said. "Everybody tried to talk Damadian out of it. But he wouldn't be talked out of it."

Damadian, ignoring the nay-sayers, prevailed and embarked on a crash program to produce the larger magnet. He felt it was important to have it ready and working for display at the following year's radiological show, before FONAR was discounted in the NMR industry. Again, the lights burned late and everyone found himself working until the early-morning hours. It was an incredibly complicated project. The magnet necessary to produce a three-thousand-gauss field, it turned out, would weigh a staggering one hundred tons, compared to the ten tons that the smaller one weighed. Just moving pieces around proved exceptionally tricky. Two teams of five people were assigned to build the magnet. Each worked an eight-hour shift. They started out adhering to a five-day-a-week schedule, but before long it stretched to six days. Stutman said, "Some of us were working twenty-hour days and going home and sleeping for four hours and coming back. It was a burnout pace. There were a lot of unhappy wives. But everyone stuck with it."

One evening, Damadian was tinkering with the machine after the other employees had gone home for the night. His son, Jevan, was with him. Stutman showed up with his own son, Mark, and pitched in. They all worked until six o'clock the next morning.

Amazed by Damadian's stamina, Mark Stutman said to him, "How can you stay up and work like this?"

Damadian glanced at him and said with a straight face, "Sheer terror."

The precise details of how Damadian managed to build a three-thousand-gauss permanent magnet remain a mystery that competing companies are still trying to unravel. Damadian will not say. Thirty days before the 1982 radiological show, however, he had succeeded in getting a three-thousand-gauss magnet to work. By the week before the show, he achieved rather good head images from the machine. The dissident forces in the company were entirely silenced. The signal-to-noise ratio was greatly improved. The images revealed details never before visible.

At the Radiological Society meeting in November, once again held in McCormick Place, FONAR presented the Beta 3000. The machine created quite a stir and drew good notices from doctors who examined the images. The first installation of the Beta 3000 was at Brunswick Memorial Hospital in Amityville, Long Island, at the end of 1983. Another unit was installed at UCLA to obtain more clinical data and user expertise. Shortly thereafter, additional orders began to arrive steadily. Damadian, who had once again felt as if his neck were in the noose, now believed that FONAR's future was strewn with possibilities.

As their images got better and better, the fabulous machines became the talk of the medical world. A number of doctors asserted that their development was as important as the discovery of X-rays nearly a century ago. One physician was quoted in a newspaper report: "With CAT scan, we mapped the interstates of the body. With NMR we'll see the back alleys." NMR scanners were being looked to to perform the sort of feats that Damadian had long foreseen for them. Early NMR scanning concentrated on neurological procedures and head scans, following the path that CAT scanning took. Now extensive human-imaging studies that were being done in England and throughout the United States were demonstrating its promise in cardiac, abdominal, spinal, and pelvic studies. Research was revealing that NMR images clearly showed blood vessels and contours of brain tissue and distinguished between different types of soft tissue. Not only were doctors managing to see internal organs, they were finding it possible to monitor processes within the organs. They could see blood coursing through an artery. They could see a knee inflamed from arthritis shrinking in response to steroids. Doctors were talking about how they expected the machines to shorten presurgical hospital diagnostic evaluations, eliminate the need for many agonizing, costly, and sometimes dangerous radiographic tests (since NMR allowed doctors to see areas of the body formerly visible only after the injection of contrast agents), and, for many patients, avoid the need for diagnostic hospitalization altogether. And, of course, it was being talked about as a way to detect disease earlier, when it can best be treated, and thus to save lives that might otherwise be lost.

NMR procedures, in various clinical settings, were spreading to embrace imaging of most of the major organs and anatomical regions of the body. Neurological applications continued to represent the most active use of NMR systems. Head studies were a logical area for NMR application, because of the importance of making precise observations of pathological conditions in the brain and central nervous system and to reveal the presence of cysts, tumors, and related growths. Any cellular damage or lesion in the brain or central nervous system is generally accompanied by an increase in the water content (edema) of the damaged tissue. This edema is one of the body's defense mechanisms and is one of its most common responses to a lesion or other pathologic condition. NMR can very competently detect edema, because of the edemic cells' longer relaxation time. A study of forty patients at New York Hospital found that in thirteen of the subjects, brain lesions in the part of the head called the posterior fossa showed up clearly on NMR images but were invisible on CAT scans.

Another frequent tissue alteration that is picked up by NMR is a hemorrhage. Blood vessels and blood flow are distinguished by virtue of the fact that rapidly moving protons return relatively little signal with certain radio-frequency pulsing sequences. Therefore arteries are seen as tubular structures with low signal intensity. Flow is detectable because the characteristic variations in intensity on the images it produces can be highlighted.

What's more, a significant advantage of NMR is its ability to verify the three-dimensional structure of a lesion by sequentially imaging multiple planes along the three perpendicular axes of the body without moving the patient. This then permits reconstruction of images that can show the volume effects of the lesion. Pituitary lesions and tumors, which are very difficult to observe with CAT scans, are reliably seen in NMR pictures. Similarly, brain-stem lesions and related pathologies, which, because of the dense surrounding base in the area, don't register on a CAT scan, are seen with NMR. (An NMR image is in effect a negative of a CAT scan, because tissue and water give very strong NMR signals, while bone's response is weak. Body tissues are about 70 percent water and bone only about 10 percent water. NMR images are sharper than images from CAT scans because the different types of tissue in the body—blood, gray and white matter of the brain, heart muscle—differ significantly in their T1 and T2 readings, which a CAT scan doesn't pick up.)

Other pathologic conditions are observed with remarkable reliability with NMR, most notably multiple sclerosis, in which there is a deterioration of the fatty protective layer around the nerve tissue. While a CAT scan detects 50 percent of patients with multiple sclerosis, British scientists found that NMR detects 90 percent. Multiple sclerosis shows up in an NMR image as distinctly as a blob of white paint on a black wall.

Damadian and others believe the technology will play an important role in the diagnosis of mental disorders. A study suggested by Damadian some years ago and later demon-strated by Minkoff indicated that the water structure in the tissue in the brain is perceptibly different for manic-depressives and can be detected by NMR. Thus scanners could be used not only for diagnosis but for tracing the progress of manic-depressives as they are administered assorted therapies. Damadian believes that NMR will prove useful for schizophrenia and other mental illnesses as well. "I think it will have valuable use for hyperactive children, who to a significant degree become full-blown manic depressives as adults." A recent study has shown that NMR can detect changes in the brains of children with learning disability syndrome, suggesting for the first time that there are organic changes in the brains of these children.

Good progress was being reported with pelvis images, important in the diagnosis of prostate and bladder cancer. NMR was especially successful in this region because of the abundant natural contrast furnished by pelvic fat and by urine in the bladder and gas in the bowel. NMR measurements have also enabled noninvasive charting of cyclical changes in the female reproductive tissue, which could be helpful in studies of female infertility and other reproductive problems.

Tumors of the nasopharynx, nasal sinuses, tongue, and neck were generally clearly identified with NMR. The technology was being used to diagnose different types of tumors and masses in the chest and to differentiate vascular anomalies and aneurysms from tumors. Primary and secondary tumors of the lung were also clearly seen with NMR. In addition, comparison with CAT scans suggested that NMR was more accurate in demonstrating the extent of tumors in the chest cavity. This was because of the clear display of blood vessels, which have characteristic relaxation-time values very different from those of tumors.

Cardiac applications seemed promising, since the NMR

machine can be synchronized with the heartbeat, producing moving pictures of the beating heart. Several investigators managed to visualize left-ventricle-wall thickening (hypertrophy). In advanced cases, dilation of the heart with poor ventricular contraction was seen. Other observations were made regarding heart-wall thinning and regional dysfunction of the wall associated with myocardial infarcts. A number of diseases related to the pericardium were examined with NMR with useful results: pericardial effusion, inflammation, thickening, cysts, and tissue masses.

Many abdominal studies have focused on inflammations and diseases of the liver and kidney, such as cirrhosis and hepatitis. NMR also seemed to have a large contribution to make in the investigation of gall-bladder disorders. In tumors involving the pancreas, NMR appeared to be more accurate than ultrasound or CAT scans in the demonstration of disease.

The method was finding application in sports medicine and orthopedics. Images show the soft tissue supporting structures around bones and joints such as ligaments, tendons, and muscle in vivid detail, whereas these structures couldn't be seen at all by X-rays. The spinal cord is visualized directly for the first time, greatly reducing the need for the painful myelogram procedure.

The list went on and on. Differentiate kidney failures due to urinary obstructions. Distinguish between benign growths and carcinoma in the prostate. Assess cervical, uterine, and ovarian cancer. Screen patients with back pain and sciatica. Study the response of arthritic joints to antiinflammatory treatments. Monitor tumor response to chemotherapy and radiotherapy.

Many in the medical community—none more so than Damadian—hope that malignant tissue can be distinguished from benign tumors through the use of NMR. However, NMR is not yet that specific. A malignant tumor does appear to have a somewhat higher relaxation time than a benign tumor. However, the ranges of relaxation times were fairly wide with both types of tissue and somewhat overlapped. Hence, it would take more understanding of the biochemical behavior of these tissues and their response to NMR excitation before this type of diagnosis could be made. "I think NMR is one hundred percent effective in distinguishing cancer from normal tissue," Damadian said. "The place where there is confusion, and we acknowledge that, is when you try to distinguish cancer tissue from other diseased tissue. There is definitely an overlap. But where some would say it's worthless, I say it's useful. The combination of the chemical readings and the appearance of the lesion on the images has to make a diagnosis more accurate."

Damadian remained convinced that eventually chemical information derived by NMR scanning would allow doctors to work up a numerical scale for various diseases, so that when a patient was scanned a number could be assigned summarizing just how seriously he was afflicted. A 4.321 cancer. A 6.802 cancer.

Studies were also made using nuclei other than hydrogen for NMR spectra—such as sodium and phosphorus—in order to provide true biochemical information on the status of tissues. Phosphorus NMR spectroscopy was a particularly hot area of investigation, since phosphorus is a major component of a number of high-energy metabolic molecules such as adenosine triphosphate (ATP), phosphocreatine, sugar phosphates, and inorganic phosphates. The energy for all of life's activities derives from chemical reactions involving phosphorus, and hence it harbors important implications for the treatment of various types of heart disease, stroke, and muscle disease. It's possible that the level and reversibility of cell damage in myocardial infarctions could be ascertained by measuring phosphorus. Producing phosphorus spectra involves using the NMR technique to create a trace or graph rather than an anatomical image. The graph presents data from a localized area of the body and displays a number of peaks that illustrate the presence of molecules in the particular atom under consideration. Examining these peaks in terms of their size and relative positioning to one another (called chemical shift) and observing how they change over time provide information about metabolic changes. The sensitivity of phosphorus imaging, though, is said to be about ten thousand times worse than that of proton imaging, even using a powerful fifteen-kilogauss system. Nonetheless, Damadian, among others, is hopeful that future breakthroughs will eventually make it possible to detect NMR signals from every element and to produce a complete chemistry of the body.

In the early days of NMR use, reports were circulated of lives being saved by the machines. *The Wall Street Journal* told of a twenty-six-year-old man afflicted by intractable seizures. A CAT scan showed nothing amiss; however, an NMR image disclosed an ugly mass of fibrous tissue in the left lobe of his brain that surgeons managed to remove. *The New York Times* reported the case of a thirty-seven-year-old man plagued by inexplicable dizzy spells. He began to bump into doorframes. Doctors probed his body for six month, like detectives going over a piece of vital evidence; they attached electrodes to his head and X-rayed him three times. It seemed that cancer had to be the culprit, but it did not show up on the X-rays. The doctors could only conclude that it must be inoperable. There was virtually nothing more to do but wait as the man slowly met his fate. As a final hope, an NMR scan was done of the young man's head using the signal Damadian discovered in 1971. A tumor clearly revealed itself in the lower part of the brain. It was already the size of the core of a golf ball. Doctors were able to extract it, saving the man's life.

In 1983, NMR began to take on the dimensions of a mammoth industry. Although the federal Food and Drug Administration had not yet approved any of the machines, a step necessary for the systems to be commercially marketed and for hospitals to be reimbursed for scanning patients, manufacturers were moving quickly to advance their products and grab marketing advantages. Even without FDA approval, companies were able to sell their machines, though they had to be offered as "investigational" devices that could not be covered by insurance. The common strategy of makers was to give away their scanners—or else agree to be paid years down the road—in order to get them accepted into prestigious hospitals that would lend credence to the product.

By 1983, there were thirteen companies committed to manufacturing NMR scanners—FONAR, Technicare, General Electric, Bruker Medical Instruments, CGR Medical Corporation, Diasonics, Elscint Limited, Intermagnetics General Corporation, Oxford Research Systems, Philips Medical Systems, Picker International, Siemens Medical Systems, and Toshiba Medical Systems. All of the competing manufacturers, in Damadian's viewpoint, were infringing on his original patent, since he had not granted any of them permission to make medical scanners based on NMR technology. (Some makers were calling their machines Magnetic Resonance Imaging, or MRI, scanners to avoid the negative connotations that the word "nuclear" had attracted.) In keeping with his belief, he filed a patent-infringement suit against Technicare (the Johnson & Johnson subsidiary, with its marketing clout and savvy, had rapidly become the most prominent company in the field), which was worming its way through the legal system. Whether anything would come of it remained uncertain. Ken Abramowitz, a health-care analyst with the brokerage firm Sanford C. Bernstein, noted in an article in *Forbes*: "Patents on devices don't usually mean that much. If a patent is really revolutionary, and the market is huge, the big guys will infringe it. If it's moderately important, the technology usually evolves so rapidly that it's bypassed." Damadian would sum up his assessment of the sanctity of patents by saying, "A patent and a million dollars to sue infringers protects your invention."

In any event, by the end of 1983, according to a lengthy study of the emerging industry by the respected New York consulting and research firm Frost & Sullivan, there were seventy-two machines either operating or being installed. Another forty machines were scheduled to be put into hospitals and clinics within the next six months. (By mid-1985, the count of installed machines had approached two hundred.) "In 1983," the report said, "NMR progressed from the status of a pure research endeavor to the level of a clinical modality with a rapidly growing base of users." The report went on to assert that there had been sufficient placement of machines and enough clinical cases reported to make useful projections of the growth of the NMR market. In 1983, thirty-nine machines were sold throughout the world (twenty-eight of them in the United States), valued at $55.5 million. Frost & Sullivan's investigators estimated that sales of NMR machines would total $156.1 million in 1984 and then soar to $512.4 million in 1986 and $704.4 million in 1988. Frost & Sullivan cautioned that it was being fairly conservative in these projections, basing them on the current understanding of NMR's uses. As it happened, new uses for the devices were being discovered steadily.

While orders were written for the scanners, an interesting battle began as competing companies based their hopes of success on different magnets. Some were making resistive systems, though most companies had opted for superconducting magnets. Though resistive magnets were cheaper, it was evident from a number of factors that they would not be around for long. They suffered from low field strength and high operating cost (because of the enormous amount of electrical power they gobbled up), as well as from poorer images and longer imaging time. FONAR alone was making a permanent magnet. In 1983, FONAR also introduced a mobile scanner that could be installed on a large truck about the size of an Allied moving van. The mobile units had a magnet with a three-thousand-gauss field strength but weighing a more manageable seventeen tons. During the year, FONAR received an order for twenty-five mobile units from Universal Medical Scanners, a mobile CAT-scanning service headquartered in Florida. The first unit was delivered in January 1984 for placement at Temple University in Philadelphia.

The Frost & Sullivan report, in comparing the annual operating expenses for various NMR systems, determined that a superconducting system, depending on its field strength, would require between $40,100 and $45,500 a year in expenses for liquid helium, liquid nitrogen, and electrical power. Damadian felt the estimate was too low; his own guess was that it would cost upward of $100,000 a year to keep a superconducting scanner functioning. A permanent FONAR system would require $15,300, all of which was for electrical power. Buttressing of the floor was generally necessary for anyone buying FONAR's system, since it weighed two hundred thousand pounds, compared to twelve thousand pounds for a superconducting machine.

One of the inherent problems of installing NMR machines is in shielding surrounding areas from the powerful magnets. Ferromagnetic materials in the environment can distort the magnetic field of the system, affecting image quality. At the same time, the magnetic field can interfere with nearby mechanical or electrical devices, such as nuclear cameras or pacemakers. At some installations, high magnetic fields have been shielded by putting steel plates in the floor and ceiling, as was done for the Philips system installed at New York's Columbia Presbyterian Hospital. The fifteen-kilogauss system was thus adequately shielded even from a bus stop that stood a mere thirty feet from the machine. Radio-frequency shielding is another worry, and it is necessary to isolate the radio signals from other instruments in the hospital, which could create artifacts in images. Electrosurgical knives were proving to be the worst offenders. Even devices outside the hospital, such as ordinary automobiles and lawnmowers, if they are close enough, can produce artifacts or render the NMR signal entirely useless. In all, site preparation for an NMR machine could run between a hundred thousand dollars and half a million dollars.

One of the grave concerns of hospitals was the so-called missile effect. The "fringe" field of a superconducting magnet extended well out from the NMR machine itself, some thirty-five feet, for example, from a three-thousand-gauss magnet. This fringe field caused metal objects to gain flight and become unpredictable and threatening projectiles. Hospitals worried about scalpels or oxygen tanks being launched (as they indeed were) as if driven by ghostly forces.

Among other side effects, things such as watches can be fouled up by the magnet. Doctors found that their beepers were broken when they passed near the scanners. Credit cards were erased (a problem that came to be called "carditis"). Some manufacturers recommended that hospitals use metal detectors, similar to those at airports, to reveal any metal objects people might have brought inadvertently into the scanning room. A clinic in Cleveland started using security boxes, sort of like bank vaults, for patients to stash their valuables in while being scanned.

Damadian designed his machine so that there was very little fringe field and thus no need to have the same number of shielding precautions. A demonstration videotape was made showing how a person could thrust his hand into the scanning area and balance a screwdriver on each finger. As he removes his hand, all of the screwdrivers clatter to the floor, showing the disappearance of the field. The tape also showed that if you thrust an oxygen tank into the field, you could yank it right out. Damadian continued to argue that superconducting scanners, with their tangle of operating worries, would prove to be white elephants and that the permanent magnet would ultimately prevail in the marketplace.

Why, then, were hospitals buying supercons? "Corporate marketing muscle," says Damadian. "When I go around to hospitals, doctors say to me, 'Dr. Damadian, you're asking me to believe that the combined brainpower of GE, Picker, Siemans, Technicare and Diasonics, which are all making supercons, you're trying to tell me that you're smarter than all of them?' Someone said that my answer should be that I invented two machines and they copied the wrong one."

As hospitals throughout the world studied the applications of NMR, it became apparent that the technology that seemed likely to suffer most from the emergence of the new machines was CAT scanning, which had become the most reliable window into the body. It seemed increasingly likely that NMR would eventually be catapulted to a place of eminence beyond all other diagnostic methods. As the Frost & Sullivan report said: "Certainly the CT market, which competes directly with NMR, will level off and begin to retrench from its present sales level (in the U.S.) of about $475 million (in 1983) to about $400 million in 1988. . . . The other markets . . . will probably not feel the competitive effects of NMR in the short-term. However, eventually NMR may displace certain nuclear medicine studies and possibly certain ultrasound procedures in the cardiac and abdominal area. The routine functions which are currently performed quite cost-effectively by these modalities will probably not be affected. However, NMR will be able to compete by being able to provide information from a single procedure that would otherwise require multiple individual procedures. Hence, the prospects exist in the longer term for a single NMR study to permit a primary diagnosis without a lot of other confirming studies. This represents one of the greatest challenges for NMR and offers the promise for reducing the cost of expensive diagnostics work-ups in the more complex cases."

FONAR, Technicare, Picker, and Diasonics were granted FDA market approval for their NMR scanners during 1984. General Electric received federal blessing in early 1985. NMR, once a private joke of the scientific community, was now safely on its way to reaching the man in the street and to reordering the way in which medical diagnosis was made.

SEVENTEEN

If you travel north across the rural flatness of Long Island onto Route 110 in the small town of Melville, turn down Pine Lawn Road, and, after a short way, make a hard right onto Marcus Drive, you come to a low-slung, relentlessly plain industrial complex. Across the way is the National Cemetery. Next door is Diplomat Electronics. The building is stark and unobtrusive. Only a small oval sign identifies its tenant: FONAR, an acronym that, of course, offers no inkling of what the company makes. The name thus means nothing to the drivers of the cars and delivery trucks that hurtle by on Pine Lawn Road—who might imagine that its business is zippers or perhaps hood ornaments for cars—or in fact to virtually all of the American public, and why should it? The company by now had moved from its cramped quarters in Plainview, but it still remained in corporate obscurity outside the medical community.

On a brittle, rainy morning, I met Damadian at the FONAR offices. The lobby might have been that of a budget motel. There was one chair for a visitor to languish in, and a fragile-looking secretary was busy answering a constantly trilling phone. Between calls, she was trying to cadge a quarter from someone to get either a Pepsi or a Sprite. Off in the rear, beyond the copier, was a small museum. A kind of nostalgia often drew Damadian back into this room. My eye was arrested by the big metal contraption looming in the center. You have to step around it to glimpse the wall, tacked thick with pictures. The contraption was a thick metal circle, a giant hula hoop stood on end, a crude Dunkin' Donuts sign. This was Indomitable. Damadian sometimes says that the story of his life is written in that machine.

Once Damadian had at last taken care of the usual mind-boggling assortment of problems—he likes to joke that FONAR is run by "crisis management"—I accompanied him in his car to Amityville and Brunswick Hospital, a large red brick tower that, at six hundred beds, is the biggest profit-making hospital in the country. "This will show you that we're actually scanning patients," Damadian said to me. "You're going to see real results."

Sitting behind the wheel, Damadian remarked, "You know, I once had a famous professor of chemistry say to me, 'It's not important to me who's right or who's wrong but that I'm on the side of the majority.' I couldn't believe it. He said this in dead earnest. I can't understand that. I've never been on the side of the majority."

He glanced out the side window, noted a semi booming past. He slipped into a minor panic, convinced that he was lost, then regained his bearings and realized that he was on a road he had traveled innumerable times. "Okay," he said. "I know where we are. We're going the right way."

Then he said, "One thing I've come to know about people and leopards is they never change their spots."

Of the players once active in the NMR imaging field, many have dispersed to new and sometimes quite remote situations. The last time I spoke with him, in 1984, Paul Lauterbur was still at Stony Brook trying to perfect better NMR techniques and working on such things as microscopic imaging and new mathematical algorithms for producing images; there were constant rumors of his taking a position elsewhere because of inadequate funds for his research. He complained that he was still saddled with the same magnets he had acquired nearly a decade ago, including the mistakenly made one that Peter Mansfield once referred to as "a whole-body magnet for a homunculus." He played down his rivalry with Damadian. "I don't even make a hobby of being against Raymond Damadian," he told me. "If it weren't for reporters, I wouldn't even think about him." (In 1985, I heard that Lauterbur had finally left Stony Brook to accept a position at the University of Illinois.)

Peter Mansfield was still at the University of Nottingham, where he was trying to devise even faster imaging techniques. When I last spoke with him, it was clear that he felt that his contributions to NMR had been underappreciated. "All of this, I think, underlines the point of advertising," he said. "I hate the commercial advertising on television, but the truth is it works. The people who promote themselves and advertise and blow the trumpets get heard. That's the way it is. Pity, isn't it?"

Waldo Hinshaw was in charge of magnetic resonance research and development for Technicare, and Raymond Andrew was ensconced at the University of Florida in Gainesville.

Waylan House was living in Texas and working as a consultant in medical imaging. He had grown greatly disillusioned with the activities in Lauterbur's lab. "I began to feel there was too much politics involved," he told me. "I began to feel that Raymond Damadian in particular was getting screwed. I didn't agree scientifically with all of the views he was espousing, but in my opinion he came up with the fundamental idea. He was a doctor without a lot of background in NMR. He had the tune right. Maybe he didn't have all of the words right. But he had the tune."

Donald Hollis was running the Cascade Motel in Chehalis, Washington, a town of five thousand people situated about thirty-five miles from the temperamental Mount St. Helens. Rooms were cheap—twenty-three dollars, including tax, with

HBO and Showtime in each of the thirty units. In 1978, after Hollis was appointed the director of NMR imaging in the department of radiology at Johns Hopkins, he managed to get an image of one rabbit heart and a few tubs of water, then he began to run into some conflicts. "Frankly, I had trouble working with MDs. They seemed to have a big interest in publishing things early, calling up *Time* magazine and all that. The other thing is, I'm a basic scientist and M.D.s are not basic scientists. They wouldn't want to know, well, what can we find out about the heart. They wanted to know when I can have one of those things in the operating room. I just didn't like the atmosphere." Hopkins, he said, became increasingly smitten by the idea of building a whole-body scanner. "I don't think they ever believed that Ray Damadian was not right," is how he phrased it. Hollis's father, who owned the Cascade Motel, died in 1976. When it was offered to Hollis in 1980, he quit Hopkins, took over the place, and bought a farm about a mile from it. "I raise chickens and sheep and ducks," he said. "It's about as close to perfect as can be."

Larry Minkoff was executive vice-president of FONAR, David Terry was the company's treasurer and secretary, and Joel Stutman was the vice-president for computer technology. Jason Koutcher was finishing an oncology fellowship at the Sidney Farber Cancer Institute of Massachusetts General Hospital. Then he planned to go into medical research, probably in NMR. Ken Zaner was an assistant professor in the hematology-oncology department at Mass General.

At the end of September 1982, Mike Goldsmith left FONAR and formed his own company—Goldsmith Scientific, a mail-order wholesaler of electronic components located in Manchester, New Hampshire. "It was a number of things" is how he would explain his departure. "I realized that my original goal of being able to do my research my own way would not be possible within the context of FONAR. Also,

Damadian and I had some disagreements over the direction that the company was taking. By this time, due to the pressures of the business, there was just a lack of communications between us. There was no reason for me to stay. We parted amicably, and I still have a lot of respect for the man. He's one of the most talented men I've ever met, if not the most talented." For all the tribulations he endured, through NMR Goldsmith found the financial security he was looking for. He was now a multimillionaire, though, he remarked, he didn't quite act like one—he had spent the previous day on his hands and knees trying to fix a broken toilet in his house. He has not forgotten the technology that led him to his pot of gold. "Every Saturday, without fail, I devote myself to NMR because I still love it and it's fun."

In 1982, the U.S. Naval Air Development Center in Warminster, Pennsylvania, shut down its human centrifuge lab, in which Freeman Cope worked. Its purpose had been to study potential G forces in the bodies of astronauts. By the 1980s, men had walked on the moon and the work was done. Cope was part of the support groups for the centrifuge lab; these units were gradually phased out. Scientific funding was getting drastically worse by the day, and Damadian had repeatedly beseeched Cope to come to FONAR and do as he pleased, but he just as repeatedly said no. "He had this idea in his head of being the unspoiled university scholar, even though he wasn't in a university, and he couldn't come to terms with entering industry," Damadian said. Finally, in October 1982, unbeknownst to Damadian, the Navy informed Cope that his work was over; he would have to vacate his lab, abandon his equipment, and move to a small room, his funding terminated. He attempted to squeeze his multiton NMR magnets into the cramped office, without success. On or about October 10, Freeman Cope, presumably despondent over the decision, killed himself. Damadian and his wife drove to his funeral in tears.

We went past Brunswick Hospital, windshield wipers beating furiously, and pulled up alongside a newish building. We parked outside the entrance and walked in. The building housed the first freestanding nuclear magnetic resonance clinic in the country and was owned as a partnership by two radiologists, Frederic Bertino and Benjamin Stein. Beyond the reception area was another chamber where a studious-looking technician sat before a computer console that boasted a tiny video monitor. After some friendly greeting, the technician placidly went back to his work. He ran his eye from the computer controls to the video screen. A swirl of fellow technicians, all of them wearing the obligatory white lab smocks, shuffled in and out, communicating in monosyllables. A partition, most of it glass, separated this chamber from a larger space almost entirely occupied by an immense machine: the first Beta 3000 to be sold. The price was a million and a half dollars, the most expensive piece of medical equipment on the market.

A pale, plump woman who appeared to be in her early sixties was lying in a supine position on a narrow orange mattress that moved along a conveyor belt and eased in and out of the gaping hole. The technician explained that the ventricle of her brain was being scanned. It was swollen. Every few minutes, pictures materialized on the miniature video screen, snapshots of the interior of her head.

Inside the scanner, a patient feels nothing but does hear sporadic noises. At least one person has compared the sound to what one might hear while folded into a garbage can with someone pounding on the outside of it with a stick. Some weeks later, I was given a head scan on a FONAR machine at Montvale Medical Imaging in Montvale, New Jersey. I was relieved of my watch and my wallet (to protect my credit cards) before being escorted into the scanning room. I lay down on the bed, my head encased in a cushion and my knees propped up above a small pillow. Masking tape was wrapped over my forehead to help keep my head still. The bed was then shoved deep inside the magnet. I had heard that a fair number of patients complain of claustrophobia while being scanned by an NMR machine, and I then understood why. It's a tight fit. It was as if I'd crawled into a sewer pipe.

When the imaging began, I heard a thump-thump-thump noise, which sounded to me like a stuttering car engine starting up. The noise was the pulsing magnetic field. Then the sound ceased. The signals returning from the hydrogen atoms in my head were being converted into a picture. The engine stuttered again so that another picture could be taken. After a while, the scanning process became totally relaxing. A technician told me that one recent patient had been lulled to sleep inside the machine.

We watched in silent fascination as the woman was shifted into new positions. "The current through-put for a patient to do a scan is forty-eight to sixty minutes," Damadian remarked. "We'd do maybe forty-five images of that particular part of the body. We're trying to get the through-put down so we can do a patient in a half hour."

The only patients that were currently being excluded from NMR machines, Damadian told me, were those with heart pacemakers (a magnetic field higher than five gauss fouls up their rhythm), those with surgical clips in their heads (if magnetic, they might move), and those with steel implants (they foul up images). The cost was six hundred and fifty dollars for a scan at Brunswick; some other hospitals were charging even more. Prices, though, were expected to come down as the popularity of the technology spread.

Later, the cheerful technician brought out packets of other

images to show Damadian and me. Some were pictures of the head of a young woman. Damadian expressed delight at the clarity of detail in the images. Tiny white blobs, like lights, were scattered in the brain. "They're lesions surrounding the ventricles that are common in multiple sclerosis," Damadian said. The woman, the technician added, had been diagnosed, for the first time, as having multiple sclerosis after being scanned. Hearing such stories, it was little wonder that a joke making the rounds at a number of hospitals was that NMR actually stands for "No More Radiologists." We looked at images of another woman's head. The lights were much larger than those in the previous image, so huge that the woman's brain seemed to turn into one bulb. Hers was a far more severe case of multiple sclerosis. "Gee, that's really dramatic," Damadian said. "And really sad."

Two divisions had by then been formed at FONAR. One was FONAR Industrial, intended to conceive and market industrial applications of the technology; Damadian had not yet made any deals, though he had been talking with corporations about some ideas he had and preferred to remain mum on the subject. The other division, Advanced Medical Diagnostic, operated scanning clinics, the first of which opened in Melbourne, Florida, at the end of 1984. In the early years, like most high-technology companies forging a way in a new product area, FONAR racked up multimillion-dollar losses. Development costs were heavy and sales, of course, were modest to nil. By the middle of 1985, however, the company was approaching the break-even point and seemed to be on sure footing. Sales had grown from zero in 1983 to $5 million in 1984 to $10.5 million in 1985. Some forty FONAR machines had been sold and about fifteen installed. One had been sold to West Germany, another to Red China. The latest price was $1.648 million.

"My real dream," Damadian said, "is to have FONAR scanning clinics all over the country. I'd like to have a thousand of them, just like McDonald's. So if you didn't feel well, you'd just walk into one of them and be scanned and diagnosed on the spot. Then you'd go to a doctor to be treated. I have another ambition. The machine could follow a person from cradle to grave. When you're born, you'd get a scan, and every few years you'd be scanned again and the chemical analysis would be stored in a computer and thus it could tell you if your chemical signals were headed in the wrong direction. We could then suggest this or that change in your life-style or your diet, or perhaps prescribe some drugs before the circumstances turned into something serious. Then I think this will be just like Bones McCoy on *Star Trek*."

Before many more years, Damadian believes, checking up on your health will be no more onerous or complex a chore than having some passport photos snapped at Woolworth's. "In ten to fifteen years," he likes to say, "we'll be able to step into a booth—they'll be in shopping malls or department stores—put a quarter in it, and in a minute it'll say you need some Vitamin A, you have some bone disease over here, your blood pressure is a touch high, and keep a watch on that cholesterol."

Ultimately, Damadian even imagines that his big Dunkin' Donuts sign might be able to slay cancer. There is no absence of therapeutics to kill cancer tissue. What is missing, though, are therapies that destroy cancer tissue but don't harm surrounding normal tissue at the dose level necessary for regression. To use a superficial example, you could take a bursomatic torch and burn to ashes the cancer but you'd also probably kill the patient. Years ago, Damadian did some experimentation with phosphorus signals using NMR. The phosphorus nucleus is located in key molecules within the cell likely to have a role in the cancerous change, particularly nucleic acid. Damadian found that there were certain frequencies in a phosphorus spectrum that were specific to cancerous tissue. Irradiation at these radio frequencies would be absorbed only by the cancerous tissue; the normal tissue would ignore it.

He explained his idea, still no more than an untested theory. "You would set the cancer frequency, and it would be picked up only by the tumor. Then I would increase the amplitude of the transmitter way above the energy I used for diagnosis and pump the energy into the cancer-specific tissue. Then it would destroy the cell. Now, a problem I ran into was, well, how much energy does the nuclear magnetic frequency absorb? If the energy is tiny, then too small an amount would be soaked up to cook the cell. As I found out, there wasn't enough energy to heat the cell. That means that there may not be enough energy to kill it. However, there's another way to look at it. I didn't necessarily have to heat up all the water in the cell. I could heat the atomic nucleus and raise it to a very, very high spin temperature. If that is done, the heated atom could disturb other atoms it's bonded to and damage the molecule. The molecule would become unstable. If you do that with a key molecule—like DNA—then the cell would still die."

"It's a long shot," he continued, "but I think it can be done."

As we pulled away from Brunswick, we talked about money. Damadian has derived considerable financial reward from his discovery. He holds stock in FONAR worth (depending on the stock market's temperament) something on the order of forty million dollars. Yet he has not become susceptible to the more insidious temptations of wealth. For seven years, he has lived in the same modest dark brown, shingled ranch house perched on a small hill on a leafy street in nearby

Plainview. About the only thing he has done with his new-found wealth, he told me, is buy a car after his old one conked out going up to Vermont. What's more, he has given away large sums to his church and to a Christian ranch in Alberta, Canada, that his sons visited. "The one thing the money's done for me," he told me, "is put me beyond the fear of financial hardship for my family and me."

His preoccupation is still his work. He hasn't played tennis more than a few times in years. His violin sits under the bed, unused. For exercise, he has a walking machine at home that he uses for about forty-five minutes in the morning. He has tried to spend more time with his children, Timothy, Jevan, and Keira, and has made some progress. "I think he's mellowed out," Donna Damadian told me. "It takes more for him to get annoyed. When we first got married, he used to get really annoyed if the telephone was dusty. He would say, 'If you could just dust the telephone, I wouldn't notice the dust in this place so much.' I haven't heard that, I'm happy to report, for a good long time."

As we drove along, Damadian fell into a ruminative mood. "Lots of people try to suppress breakthroughs," he said. "They lose money and reputations. It's treacherous and undermines research. A lot of professors have been buried by it. I was tolerated somewhat better because I was asserting not that I was going to cure cancer but diagnose it. If I asserted I was going to cure it, I would have probably been exterminated, figuratively. My general opinion of why we have had cancer around for the last fifty or seventy years is because we've suppressed the cure."

He said he was disappointed that his ion-exchange theory of the cell, his new concept of life, was as ignored by the scientific community as when he first proposed it. His friend Gilbert Ling continues to toil in obscurity. But he felt that NMR would help prove him correct. "Why is the NMR signal higher in cancer than normal tissue? Who knows the answer to that other than me?" he said. "In a cancer cell, others explain the elevated T1 because there's more water. This is true in most diseases. But the real event that's taking place is that the water is becoming more and more disorganized and less structured in the cell, less icelike, as Cope would say."

We arrived back at the FONAR offices and sat in the conference room, on chrome-tubed, executive-style chairs. It was about ten and neither of us had eaten. Elsewhere in the company, pizza had arrived for some late owls, and Damadian, sniffing its aroma, managed to wheedle a couple of slices. He wolfed his down with big bites, then continued speaking.

Talking about motivation, he said, "I saw an old interview with Maurice Chevalier on the television the other night, and he was asked what was the one thing responsible for his success and he said honesty. That's pretty much the way I feel. You've got to be honest. Not only to others, but honest to yourself."

He was quiet for a bit and looked somewhat puzzled. "A friend of mine told me once, 'Why, Raymond, you know how to recognize a pioneer?' I asked how. 'Why, he's the guy with all the arrows in his back.'"

He paused and ran his fingers in a rapid sweep through his white hair. Nibbling on his nails, he said, "Nobody else is going to cure cancer. So I'm going to have to do it. And I will. I used to be convinced that it was beyond the capacity of one individual to do it, because the forces opposing it were too much. But I think a corporation can do it, because those forces can't crush it the way they can a single scientist. So I feel confident. I feel confident that I'm going to do it."

In the pale wash of the lighting, he talked on, animatedly, about disease and about the cell, about how whoever didn't agree with his ideas could step out of the way. The phone rang—some radiologist calling from a distant city. Damadian filled him in on the quality of the latest pictures and brought him up to date on some recent sales. It was pretty obvious that he would be on for a while. It was almost midnight. The machine was still his life.

INDEX

INDEX

INDEX

INDEX

INDEX

247

INDEX

INDEX

T2 (spin-spin relaxation), 24, 25, 30, 84, 219
tongue, tumors of the, 220
Toshiba Medical Systems, 224
Tufts University, 95
tumor detection and treatment monitoring, NMR scanners for, 218, 220, 221, 223–24
see also cancer; cancer cells
"Tumor Detection by Nuclear Magnetic Resonance," 31–32, 53, 54, 62

ultrasound procedures, 228–29
U.S. Air Force, 11, 14
U.S. Army Chemical Center, 56
United States Naval Air Development Center, 21, 234
United University Professors, 151
Universal Medical Scanners, 226
University Hospital, 83
University of Aberdeen, 100, 215
University of California:
    at Berkeley, 11–12
    at Los Angeles, 217
    at San Francisco, Radiologic Imaging Laboratory at, 215
University of Chicago, 47, 91
University of Florida, Gainesville, 232
University of Illinois, 232
University of Mexico, 212
University of Milan, 212
University of Nottingham, 63–65, 99, 190, 196, 232
University of Pittsburgh, 57
University of Puget Sound, 53
University of Wisconsin, 47, 147
urine, 8

Vanderbilt Engineering School, 160, 161

Varian Associates, 53
Vickers, Donald, 31, 33, 58, 59–60, 61, 139, 192–93

Walker sarcoma, 29, 30
Walker Scientific, 122, 123
Wall Street Journal, The, 223
Warner-Lambert, 71
Washington University, St. Louis, 8
water softener, 12–13
Watson, Jack, 160
Watson, Judith, 160
West Germany, 237
Westhampton Bath and Tennis Club, 49
Westinghouse Corporation, 68, 121
Westinghouse Science Talent Search Awards, 46
West Side Tennis Club, 40, 42, 43
Worcester Polytechic Institute, 109

X-ray equipment, 37, 95, 217, 221
    CAT scanning, 95–96, 100, 217, 218, 219, 220, 223, 228

Yajko, Paul, 22, 28–29, 57
Yale University, 47, 91
Yazedjian, Haig, 38–39
Yazedjian, Odette, *see* Damadian, Odette
Yeshiva University, 48
Young, Ina, 100

Zaner, Ken, 83, 91, 93, 233
zeugmatography, 61, 63, 101